Aspects of Prehistory

Grahame Clark

ASPECTS OF PREHISTORY

UNIVERSITY OF CALIFORNIA PRESS

Berkeley, Los Angeles, London 1970

University of California Press
Berkeley and Los Angeles, California
University of California Press, Ltd.
London, England
Copyright © 1970, by
The Regents of the University of California
ISBN: 0-520-01584-3
Library of Congress Catalog Card Number: 73-94989
Printed in the United States of America

Contents

Illustrations

vii

Ostrava-Petrkovice, Czechoslovakia; (b) bronze relief "The Back II" by Henri Matisse

FIGURES

Preface

The worldwide application of prehistoric research has made it possible for the first time to visualize the antecedents and emergence both of preliterate societies and of all the various civilizations of men. No one can survey so vast a panorama without meditating both on its meaning for ourselves and on the processes by which prehistory has unfolded. One effect of the new picture of the past that has recently come into view has been to narrow down and even in some respects eliminate the gap between the universal concepts of science and technology and the parochial limitations of histories based on the

written records of particular civilizations. In world prehistory all men whatever their recent cultural status—
and large parts of the world remained prehistoric down
to the nineteenth century—share a common past documented by millions of tangible fossils. But prehistory
does more than provide a common area of historical
awareness among men; it also removes the barrier once
thought to separate men from other animals—or at least
it helps us to understand more fully in what respects we
are animals of a unique kind. Man himself, his material
apparatus of technology, and his self-awareness manifest
in such fields as art, ethics, religion, and philosophy can
be viewed as outcomes of the same evolutionary process
by which we have long learned to account for other forms
of life and indeed for the universe as a whole. There is
no longer any valid ground for conflict between the notion that man is at one and the same time an animal and
yet potentially divine. Indeed, the record of prehistory
shows that societies of human character have been selected for survival precisely through the development of
the attributes that stem from increasing self-awareness,
attributes shared by no other animal and which men
have everywhere recognised as of god-like character.

The present book, which treats only a few of the central themes opened up by this new field of knowledge, is
the outcome of reflection following on the writing of
World Prehistory: An Outline, originally published by
Cambridge University Press in 1961 and recently revised
and largely rewritten as *World Prehistory: A New Outline*, published by the same press in 1969. Although some
of the ideas incorporated in it were adumbrated in lec-

tures delivered as William Evans Visiting Professor at
the University of Otago, New Zealand, in 1964, and as
Lewis Fry Memorial Lecturer at the University of Bris-
tol in 1967, the stimulus to develop them further came
from the invitation to serve as Visiting Professor on the
Charles M. and Martha Hitchcock Foundation on the
Berkeley campus of the University of California in 1969.
The three chapters of this book represent the substance
of the three lectures delivered at Berkeley. In preparing
these for publication, I have endeavoured to take advantage of the greater scope and precision of the printed
page without departing in any radical way from what I
sought to convey to my audience. The problem of recon-
ciling the requirements of the reader with the recollec-
tions of anyone who heard the lectures is not an easy one.
I have been able to enlarge on certain topics, but I have
sought to keep my chapters down to a length not too
much in excess of what can be conveyed in lectures. I
have been greatly helped in this by being able to provide
numerous references to the literature in the form of
footnotes.

I would like, in conclusion, to thank Vice-Chancellor
Bouwsma for the graceful manner in which he introduced my opening lecture and to express my pleasure at
being able to renew contacts with many colleagues in the
Department of Anthropology at Berkeley, as well as at
Los Angeles and Santa Barbara, from whom I have im-
bibed not merely facts but insights.

GRAHAME CLARK
Cambridge, England
September, 1969

1

The Relevance of World Prehistory

It is the past that explains everything, I say to myself. It is in our sense of the past that we find our humanity. . . . The past tells us whence we came and what we are.

GEORGE MOORE

Man has no nature; what he has is history.

ORTEGA Y GASSET

COL. BORMAN'S REPLY from Apollo 8, "there's a beautiful earth out there,"[1] conveys in a very direct and simple manner what many of us feel about our situation. We are conscious as our fathers could hardly have been that we live in one world; this world seems very small. It is not merely that in relation to outer space it is the merest speck; still more to the point is it that we can traverse continents and oceans that a few generations ago would have taken many weeks and can communicate by word and picture from one part of the globe to another in hardly any time at all. And our world and indeed the proximate regions of outer space are still shrinking. Yet the mentality even of those who in effect rule the world, not to mention the ideas and passions of mankind in general, still reflect the limitations of a previous age when nations and even civilizations were still to a large degree self-sufficient.

It is in this context of broad concern that we may now consider the relevance of world prehistory. The study of world prehistory is capable of opening up historical perspectives of which we stand in dire need if we are to come to terms with the world in which ineluctably we have to live and in which we may still hope to perpetuate our species. In making this suggestion I am by no means

---

[1] Quoted from the transcript of the dialogue between earth and the spacecraft Apollo 8. The point has since been made even more emphatically by the first men to land on the moon.

urging that the study of prehistory stands in any need of extraneous justification, but merely that it has something to contribute to our awareness of the basic problems of our time. Some measure of freedom from the constrictions of present time and place is inherent in and peculiar to the human condition. William R. Dennes expressed this very clearly in a paper read before the Philosophical Union at Berkeley in 1941 when he maintained that "human beings emancipate themselves from the tyranny of the present and the local, share the experience of other ages and of other nations, preserve and interpret their own observations, consider possibilities unbounded in range, predict the future and guide themselves in shaping it."[2]

One of the prime ways they have achieved this emancipation has been by exploring their own origins and establishing their own identity, first through the written word and latterly through archaeology and cognate disciplines by means of which it has been possible to extend the range of historical awareness far back into prehistoric times. The study of prehistory stands in no more need of justification than exploration of the physical nature and mathematical properties of the universe, the investigation of all the multifarious forms of life, or for that matter the practice of the arts or the cultivation of speculative philosophy. Each in its own way enlarges the range of human experience and enriches the quality of human life. We have it on the authority of the English

[2] "Conceptions of Civilization: Descriptive and Normative," in V. F. Lenzen et al., *Civilization* (Berkeley and Los Angeles: University of California Press, 1959), p. 171.

historian George Macaulay Trevelyan that "Man's evolution is far more extraordinary than the first chapter of Genesis used to lead people to suppose. Man's history, pre-historic, ancient, medieval and modern, is by far the most wonderful thing in the Universe of which any news has come through to us."[3]

Before coming to grips with our topic it is worth emphasising that the possibility of considering the history of man in the perspective of world prehistory is a very recent one: the very notion of prehistory as we understand it is only four or five generations old,[4] and it has only been possible to think in precise terms of world prehistory during the few years since the technique of radiocarbon dating (see p. 38) has been applied to the dating of deposits in widely separated parts of the earth.[5] Archaeology, the most important of the several disciplines used to extend historical knowledge beyond the confines of written documents, was first developed, if only to a limited degree, among the Chinese under the powerful impulse of historical scholarship rooted ulti-

[3] G. M. Trevelyan, *History and the Reader* (London, 1945), pp. 24–25.

[4] Sir John Lubbock's *Prehistoric Times, as Illustrated by Ancient Remains, and the Manners and Customs of Modern Savages,* published in 1865, was the first major work to include the whole range from the Paleolithic to the Iron Age.

[5] Oswald Menghin made a brave attempt to cover Stone Age material from the whole world in his *Weltgeschichte der Steinzeit,* published in Vienna in 1931. But this book, which was marked by a highly schematic treatment, stopped short at the Stone Age and made only nominal mention of material outside Africa, Asia, and Europe. In writing *World Prehistory* I received immense help from radiocarbon dating, more especially in the 1969 edition.

mately in respect for ancestors.[6] In the West archaeology developed initially as part of the process of rediscovering Classical antiquity, but its main impulse has undoubtedly come from the upsurge of national feeling that has everywhere ushered in the modern age.[7] Even so, in the context of European civilization, antiquarian and archaeological studies were long subservient to literary scholarship. In the context of his day William Camden (1551–1623) was fully justified in distinguishing three eras of past time, nicely graded in accordance with the reliability of surviving written sources:[8]

[6] See Dr. Cheng Te-k'un in his *Archaeology of China*, vol. 1, p. xvi. The beginning of archaeology in that country dates back to early in the Han period when, toward the end of the second century B.C., Ssŭ-ma Ch'ien, court historian of the dynasty, traveled widely in order to study ancient remains in different parts of China. In the course of these travels he became the first scholar to locate the ancient Shang capital near the modern An-yang, still the key site for the period. During the Sung period, connoisseurs had rubbings taken of early tomb reliefs; examples displayed in the Palace Museum at Taipei from the royal collections betray an extremely high standard of execution and compare favourably with the brass rubbings currently popular in England. The archaizing tendencies in bronze work and porcelains are further indications of continuing Chinese interest in ancient artifacts, a concern that is readily understandable given the respect for ancestors deep-seated in Chinese culture.

[7] See Grahame Clark's *Archaeology and Society* (London: 1st ed., 1939, chap. 7; 3rd ed., 1957, chap. 8). For a fuller account, see Glyn Daniel's *Hundred Years of Archaeology* (London, 1950), and the collection of extracts assembled in his *The Origins and Growth of Archaeology* (London, 1967).

[8] Edmund Gibson's translation of Camden's *Britannia* (London, 1695), pp. vi, xxviii.

6

1. A period of History, properly so-called "because the transactions of that space are related by good Historians," a period going back as far as the First Olympiad.

2. A Fabulous period, extending from the First Olympiad back to the Deluge, so termed "because most of those Histories are fabulous, even of the Greek and Roman Authors, the learned part of the world."

3. A period of Obscurity from the Deluge to the Creation "so called from our ignorance of the transactions of those times."

Yet even Camden could hardly refrain from illustrating a monument so prominent and yet so un-Roman as Stonehenge (Fig. 1). It is significant that, even if he felt impelled to characterise the monument as *insana substructio*[9] and grieved that "the founders of this noble monument cannot be trac'd out,"[10] he nevertheless depicted several interested spectators and showed an excavation in full progress. The future lay with the spade, even if those who wielded this essential tool in the interests of archaeology were treated more as eccentrics than as men having anything useful to say about the early history of man. Yet, slowly but surely the evidence accumulated as burial mounds were dug and stray finds found their way into the cabinets of collectors and more importantly into public museums. The significance of

[9] *Britannia*, p. 94.
[10] *Britannia*, p. 95.

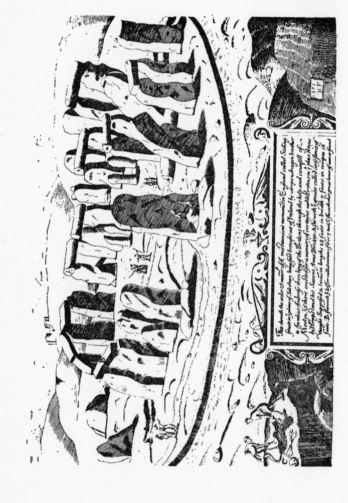

FIG. 1. Representation of Stonehenge in William Camden's *Britannia*

these institutions in the development of archaeological studies can hardly be exaggerated, since it was in these that antiquities, other than monumental structures, were first systematically studied at a time when archaeology was still largely ignored in universities. The classification of antiquities was initially undertaken and later systematically pursued as a guide to the arrangement and appreciation of museum collections.[11]

Archaeology, even systematic archaeology, was developed well before prehistory in its expanded modern sense. Of course, the early archaeologists were in some cases aware that they were delving back into a time anterior to the earliest recorded histories of their homelands; and over much of western Europe this meant that they were concerned with antiquities dating from before the Romans. Yet they were concerned with the more or less immediate antecedents of their national histories, the range of archaeology concerned with *la protohistoire* rather than with *la préhistoire*. To C. J. Thomsen, whose Three-Age System is justly regarded as a turning point in the classification of archaeological data,[12] the Stone Age of Denmark began a mere three thousand years ago. Even more significant in some ways is the fact that the father of British speleology, Dean Buckland, should have

[11] The handbooks and catalogues of great museums form essential tools for the archaeologist. The first of these, C. J. Thomsen's *Ledetraad til Nordisk Oldkyndighed* (Copenhagen, 1836), prepared for the National Museum at Copenhagen, provided the first systematic classification of archaeological data.

[12] See Glyn Daniel's *The Three Ages: An Essay in Archaeological Method* (Cambridge, 1943).

dedicated his book published in 1823 to the Lord Bishop of Durham and entitled it *Reliquiae Diluvianae: Or, Observations on the Organic Remains Contained in the Caves, Fissures and Diluvial Gravel, and on Other Geological Phenomena, Attesting the Action of an Universal Deluge.* Thomsen, Buckland, and their contemporaries were confined as late as the early decades of the nineteenth century to traditional ideas about man's context in time.

The concept of *La Préhistoire,* the idea that mankind had developed over immensely long periods of time before ever adopting settled life, did not emerge until men had become fully aware of the antiquity of their own species, which could not happen so long as the notion of a fixed order of nature prevailed. It is difficult for us to understand how firmly established this doctrine was unless we realise that it was held in place by two of the most powerful forces of the day, namely Biblical fundamentalism and mathematical thought. As Stephen Toulmin and June Goodfield have noted,[13] the year fixed upon by Archbishop Ussher for the Creation, 4004 B.C., was arrived at on the basis of an initial calculation by Martin Luther corrected by none other than the astronomer Johann Kepler. That an astronomer should have concerned himself with checking the date of the Crucifixion by reference to an established cycle of solar eclipses is particularly revealing. The first scientific revolution, that of the sixteenth and seventeenth centuries, was basically mathematical. Since mathematical propositions

[13] *The Discovery of Time* (London, 1965), p. 76.

were held at that time to exist in a kind of temporal
vacuum, it was generally accepted that "the laws govern-
ing nature in the present epoch were . . . those which had
governed it at all times." In this respect there was no
quarrel between the mathematical scientists and the up-
holders of fundamentalism; between them they formed
a barrier to evolutionary thought.

The attack on the fixed state of nature came on two
converging fronts. On the one hand geologists, both on
the European continent and in Britain, found it difficult
to reconcile their observations with the brief period of
time allowed them by the conventional chronology.
For instance, J. E. Guettard's recognition in 1751 that
the peaks of the Puy de Dôme were of volcanic origin
was soon followed by parallel observations in other regions; it seemed hard to accept that all these phases of
mountain-building could have been accomplished in
the short time allowed by Archbishop Ussher. Even more
challenging was the elaborate sequence of rock strata
distinguished by the Saxon geologist A. G. Werner on
the basis of empirical observations made by generations
of miners; and the Scottish geologist James Hutton
(1726–1797) felt obliged from his study of geological
processes to infer that an indefinite length of time
was implied by the formation of the earth. Ironically,
Charles Lyell appealed to the mathematical principle of
uniformitarianism when in 1830 he maintained in his
Principles of Geology that rock formations must have
been formed by forces still to be observed in action; that
no catastrophe or intervention was required to account
for what geologists could now see; and that in conse-

quence long periods of time must have been involved for the gradual transformations.

The other line of attack, that of biology, was closely linked with geology for the simple reason that changes in the nature of organic fossils from one layer to another provided one of the most obvious keys to geological stratigraphy. Conversely, it is a notable fact that it was the French naturalist Buffon (1707–1788), director of what was to prove the prototype of the Jardin des Plantes in Paris, who first published precise estimates of the age of the earth that far exceeded that envisaged by Archbishop Ussher. Another Frenchman, Jean B. Lamarck (1744–1829), seized on the fact that the older the rocks, the simpler the organisms contained in them in fossil form, and from there went on to argue that more complex forms of life were linked by descent from older, simpler ones. Although in making this suggestion he had been forestalled by the English thinker, Erasmus Darwin (1731–1802), grandfather of Charles, Lamarck can claim credit for having published the first evolutionary family tree in his *Zoological Philosophy* (1809). What he failed to accomplish and what was to remain undone for around half a century was to provide a convincing explanation for the process of evolution.

It is amply established that already before the end of the eighteenth century men of science were becoming accustomed to the notion that the earth itself and the various forms of life which it supported had assumed their present forms gradually by natural processes over immensely long periods of time. In this context it is not difficult to understand why the scheme of archaeological classification proposed by C. J. Thomsen should have been basically transformist, resting as it did on the premise that men advanced by taking into use progressively more effective raw materials. Yet it required something as dramatic as the publication of *The Origin of Species*, in which Charles Darwin offered natural selection as a convincing hypothesis for evolution and not least the controversy aroused by this awoke men to the full implications of evolutionary doctrine. The effect of this theory was, indeed, electrifying. Whereas in the lifetime of Dean Buckland what we now recognize to have been highly significant discoveries relating to Paleolithic man were either ignored or speciously explained away,[14] men now came to recognise in the light of Thomas Huxley's pronouncement[15] that it was necessary to "extend by long epochs the most liberal estimate that has yet been made of the Antiquity of Man," that discoveries of a similar nature were no longer to be regarded as anomalous but rather as meaningful necessities. In the light of the Darwinian revolution, the vision of men like Aubrey, Stukeley, Lhwyd, or Thomsen appears hardly less constricted

[14] E.g. the discovery announced by John Frere to the Society of Antiquaries on June 22, 1797 (*Archaeologia*, XII, 204) of flint implements from a deposit at Hoxne, Suffolk, that tempted him "to refer them to a very remote period indeed, even beyond that of the present world" caused very little remark at the time. Similarly, Dean Buckland, the discoverer, felt constrained to account (*Reliquiae Diluvianae*, p. 87) for what we now recognise to have been a Paleolithic burial in the cave of Paviland in terms of the builders of a nearly British "camp."

[15] T. H. Huxley, *Man's Place in Nature and Other Anthropological Essays* (London, 1911), p. 208.

than that of Archbishop Ussher[16] or of Dr. Johnson.[17]
The doctrine of evolution was indeed crucial and not
merely for extending more than a hundred-fold the
temporal duration of human history, but still more for
bringing man and his works firmly within the scope of
the natural order. It implied that all men of whatever
standing had reached their present situation as a result
of a process of transformation comparable to that which
has shaped the earth and all the varied forms of animal
and plant life. The life of man no longer began when he
first laid foundations for the earliest literate civilizations
on earth; it was no more sufficient to recover the immediate background to history. It was now necessary to trace
the very processes of hominization, to see how certain
hominids attained the status of men and how these men
progressed to the threshold of civilized life. To achieve
this was going to involve an immensely long process of
retrieving and interpreting data from deposits derived
from every stage of the Pleistocene and from every part
of the world from which it was available.

A significant landmark in prehistoric studies was the
appearance in 1865 of Sir John Lubbock's *Pre-historic
Times, as Illustrated by Ancient Remains, and the Manners and Customs of Modern Savages*, a work that con-

[16] James Ussher, Archbishop of Armagh (1581–1656), opined
that the world began in 4004 B.C. See his *Annales Veteris et Novi
Testamenti*, 2 vols., 1650–1654.

[17] Dr. Johnson was prepared to state dogmatically, "All that is
known of the Ancient State of Britain is contained in a few
pages. . . . We can know no more than what the old writers have
told us." Quoted from the 1859 edition of James Boswell's *The
Life of Samuel Johnson, LL.D.*, vol. 3, chap. 12, p. 224.

tinued to appear for nearly half a century, the seventh
and last edition being published in 1913. The book was
notable not merely for including under one cover a
range of materials extending from handaxes from diluvial gravels up to Iron Age runes, but also for dividing the
Stone Age into two fundamental divisions: the Paleolithic, marked by a hunting and gathering economy, the
presence of extinct animals, and the occurrence of exclusively chipped flint; and the Neolithic, defined by the
practice of farming, the manufacture of pottery, the
polishing of flint stone axes, and the absence of bones of
extinct animals. The book summarised data contributed
by two distinct types of prehistorian. On the one hand
there were those of more scientific bent, concerned with
the more remote prehistory of man, anterior to or geo-
graphically remote from early centers of civilization,
men who were most liable to take a world view and who,
incidentally, generally followed the forward flow of time.
On the other were those concerned more especially with
the antecedents and origins of particular civilizations,
men often having a more humanistic approach with
strong local attachments and who commonly preferred
to work backward from the historic into the prehistoric
past. It was the latter who carried forward a line stemming in unbroken succession from the sixteenth and
seventeenth centuries, whereas the true prehistorians
were products of the Darwinian era. This division still
survives within the broad fellowship of prehistorians as
this exists in the English-speaking world.[18] Although

[18] See Grahame Clark, "Perspectives in Prehistory," *Proceedings of the Prehistoric Society*, 25 (1959), 1–14.

masked to some degree by the common aims of the subject, it is still sufficiently alive to stimulate discussion and heighten tension; and it tends to separate those who explain prehistory in anthropomorphic or evolutionary terms (see p. 60).

Furthermore, both the main lines of approach to prehistory, together with the principal methods—archaeological, geological, and biological—were initially developed in Europe and only later, in many regions quite recently, applied to other continents. The driving forces in this movement differed to some degree in each of the two segments of prehistory. In the case of the later periods these have included national and patriotic feeling and on the other hand a scholarly devotion to the study of particular civilizations. It is no accident that archaeology grew up in the continent that gave birth to the nation-state. Likewise it was the concentration of wealth and learned institutions in western Europe that accounts for the lead taken by scholars of that region in laying the foundations for the specialised study of the great civilizations of antiquity,[19] and at the same time

[19] Many European countries and in due course the U.S. sought to further knowledge of the archaeology of the lands from which Western Civilization has drawn inspiration by founding societies and setting up institutes and schools, part of the object of which was to cooperate with and assist the nations of host countries in the recovery of their early history and prehistory. The British effort, to give one example, included the Palestine Excavation Fund (1865) and the British School of Archaeology in Jerusalem (1920), the Egypt Exploration Fund (1883), the British School of Archaeology at Athens (1886), the British School at Rome (1901) and the Society for the Promotion of Roman Studies (1911), the British

that gave scholars the opportunity to investigate the origins of these civilizations and explain their impact on adjacent territories in terms of archaeology. Thus it was that Europeans both laid bare the foundations of their own national histories and in the long run the prehistoric origins of European civilization as a whole—as was first demonstrated by Gordon Childe[20] in his *Dawn of European Civilization* (1925)—and, at the same time, illumined the antecedents and measured the influence of the ancient civilizations of Egypt, Mesopotamia, the Indus Valley, and China.

The scholars of western Europe and, in due course, of North America were particularly concerned with gaining more knowledge about the civilizations to which they felt most indebted culturally. In each case, they began with the archaeology of a particular historic period and worked backward in time. Thus the first archaeologists to concern themselves in modern times with Greece concentrated first on the material setting of the classical

School of Archaeology in Iraq (1932), the British Institute of Archaeology at Ankara (1949), and the British Institute of Persian Studies (1961).

[20] Gordon Childe came to Britain from the University of Sydney, Australia. He was fascinated by the peculiar quality of European civilization. After a brief period at Oxford he spent some time in Central Europe where he obtained a firsthand grasp of the prehistoric archaeology of a key area. He became first professor to occupy the Abercromby chair of Prehistoric Archaeology at Edinburgh in 1927 and in 1946 moved to London to direct the Institute of Archaeology. He died in Australia. For an account of his life see the obituary by Stuart Piggott in the *Proceedings of the British Academy*, 1958, pp. 305–312.

texts. The revelation of the Bronze Age background[21] was initiated by Heinrich Schliemann when he began to dig at Mycenae in 1876 and by the campaigns at Knossos (1899–1932) by Arthur Evans that resulted in the revelation of Minoan civilization. The decipherment by Ventris and Chadwick of inscriptions in Linear B on clay tablets from Pylos and Knossos showed that the Late Bronze inhabitants of Greece were already speaking a Greek tongue. As archaeologists dug deeper into the soil of the Greek mainland and of Crete, it became evident that settled life was far older even than the earliest Minoan. At Knossos, Evans found deposits relating to early peasant communities directly underlying the palace remains that by their mere thickness indicated an impressive duration. Meanwhile, shortly after Evans began to dig in Crete, Tsountas found traces of settled communities of comparable age on the Greek mainland at Sesklo (1901) and Dhimini (1903); and by 1912 A. J. B. Wace and M. S. Thompson were able to publish a convincing account of the Neolithic settlement of Thessaly.[22] The full antiquity of settled life in Greece was not made apparent until renewed excavation and the application of radiocarbon dating had been carried out since the Second World War in Thessaly, the Peloponnesus, West Macedonia, and Crete—research which made it apparent

---

[21] A. J. B. Wace, *Mycenae: An Archaeological History and Guide* (Princeton, 1949); Lord William Taylour, *The Mycenaeans* (London, 1964); M. Ventris and J. Chadwick, *Documents in Mycenaean Greek* (Cambridge, 1956); Arthur Evans, *The Palace of Minos* (London, 1921–1928); and R. W. Hutchinson, *Prehistoric Crete* (London, 1962).

[22] *Prehistoric Thessaly* (Cambridge).

that settled life had existed in Greece for some three millennia before the rise of Minoan civilization.[23] Finally, excavations in the caves of Asprochaliko and Kastritsa near Ionnina between 1964–1968,[24] together with more sporadic discoveries elsewhere, made it plain that Greece had been inhabited at least as far back as the Middle Paleolithic.

Much the same thing happened when archaeologists turned to Egypt. The recovery of the Rosetta stone by the French expedition to the Nile in 1799, by facilitating the decipherment of heiroglyphic inscriptions, gave an immense impetus to the study of remains of the Pharaonic period; and it was on these that scholars concentrated exclusively for many decades. French scholars played a leading part in the development of Egyptology, but American, British, German, Italian, and of course Egyptian workers have also contributed in very important ways in this field. It was not until the Scotsman, Flinders Petrie, began his campaign of excavating Predynastic cemeteries in 1890 that knowledge began to accumulate about the immediate antecedents of Dynastic Egypt.[25]

[23] V. Milojčić et al., *Die Deutschen Ausgrabungen auf der Argissa-Magula in Thessalien* (Bonn, 1962); S. S. Weinberg, "The Stone Age in the Aegean," *Cambridge Ancient History*, fasc. 36 (1965); D. P. Theochares, *The Dawn of Thessalian Prehistory* (Volos, 1967); R. J. Rodden, *Proceedings of the Prehistoric Society*, 28 (1962), 267–288; J. D. Evans, *Annals of the British School of Archaeology at Athens*, 59 (1964), 132–240.

[24] E. S. Higgs, *Proceedings of the Prehistoric Society*, 30 (1964), 199–244; 32 (1966), 1–29; 33 (1967), 1–29.

[25] Petrie's work has been well summarised by V. G. Childe in chap. 4 of his *New Light on the Most Ancient East* (London, 1934, 1935, and 1952).

Convincing evidence for still earlier settled life in Egypt had to wait on the resumption of archaeological exploration following the Second World War, when Austrian and British expeditions brought to light traces of settlements and cemeteries belonging to peasant communities whose technologies were still limited almost entirely by the potentialities of stone tools.[26] At the same time, researches mainly by British prehistorians and geologists made it clear that the country had been occupied far back into the Old Stone Age.[27]

Palestine had long exercised a powerful attraction on European scholars on account of the Bible, but the first man to develop excavation systematically in this territory was Flinders Petrie largely because during antiquity it had fallen within the sphere of Egyptian hegemony. Attention was accordingly directed first to the later phases of Palestinian archaeology; excavators from many European states as well as the United States contributed to the documentation of these phases.[28] The idea that Palestine had been occupied since remote prehistoric times was not made evident until Dorothy Garrod undertook her excavation of caves in the region of Mount Carmel on behalf of the British School of Archaeology in Jerusa-

[26] G. Brunton and G. Caton-Thompson, *The Badarian Civilization* (London, 1928); G. Caton-Thompson, *The Desert Fayum* (London, 1935); H. Junker, *Anzeiger der Akademie der Wissenschaft Wien Philosophisches-Historisches Klasse* (1929–1930, 1932, 1940).

[27] G. Caton-Thompson, *The Kharga Oasis in Prehistory* (London, 1952); K. S. Sandford, *University of Chicago Oriental Institute Publications*, Nos. 18 (1934) and 46 (1939).

[28] See chap. 2 of W. F. Albright, *The Archaeology of Palestine* (London, 1949).

lem and of the American School of Prehistoric Research.[29] The gap between Mount Carmel and the peoples known to history was not adequately bridged until after the Second World War, when British, French and Israeli archaeologists recovered traces of a succession of communities ranging in their technology from transitional to full Neolithic and Bronze Age.[30]

Archaeological exploration in the territory from Anatolia to Mesopotamia and Iran was similarly directed first to the material traces of peoples identified in the ancient literatures. British, French, and German excavators concentrated on the architecture and reliefs of such civilized peoples as the Assyrians, Hittites, and Persians. Despite such pioneering work as Schliemann's at Troy and de Morgan's at Susa, little progress was made at first in recovering the protohistory or prehistory of this extensive region. Progress had to wait on the overthrow of the Ottoman Empire and the establishment each in its separate territory of successor states. The effect of the First World War was not merely to open up extensive territories to intensive research by American and European archaeologists; it was also destined to arouse lively interest in each of the new countries. By the outbreak of the Second World War much had already been done to investigate the immediate antecedents of literate civilization in each of these lands. Sumerian civilization

[29] D. A. E. Garrod and D. M. A. Bate, *The Stone Age of Mount Carmel* (Oxford, 1937).

[30] Kathleen M. Kenyon, *Digging up Jericho* (London, 1957); Diana Kirkbride, *Palestine Exploration Quarterly*, 98 (1966), 8–66; J. Perrot, *Antiquity and Survival*, 2 (1957), 90–110; M. Stekelis and T. Yizraely, *Israel Exploration Journal*, 13 (1963), 1–12.

and its immediate antecedents had been revealed by the
excavation at the hands of American, British, German,
and Iraqi archaeologists at many sites of the quality of
Ur, Tell Asmar, Tepe Gawra, Warka, and Al'Ubaid in
Mesopotamia. Meanwhile, at Tell Halaf in southern
Turkey, German archaeologists had dug back to levels
of comparable age, as French ones had at Ras Shamra in
Syria and Sialk in Iran. The best summary of the situation as it appeared at the outbreak of the Second World
War is still that given by Gordon Childe in his *New
Light on the Most Ancient East* published in 1952. The
next step, the attempt to trace the beginnings of settled
life in these territories, was taken with the return of
peace. Among key excavations were those undertaken on
either side of the Iraqi-Iranian frontier by American excavators, notably by Braidwood at Jarmo,[31] Solecki at
Shanidar,[32] and Hole and Flannery at Ali Kosh;[33] also by
the Danes at Tepe Guran,[34] and the Japanese at Bakun.[35]
During the same era the Russians, by their excavations
at Djeitun in Turkmenia,[36] amplified and carried further the work done by an American expedition at
Anau earlier in the century; and the American Carle-
ton Coon carried out important excavations on the Cas-

[31] R. Braidwood and Bruce Howe, *Prehistoric Investigations in
Iraqi Kurdistan* (Chicago, 1960).

[32] *Science* (1963), pp. 179–193.

[33] *Proceedings of the Prehistoric Society*, 33 (1967), 147–206.

[34] J. Meldgaard, P. Mortensen, and H. Thrane, *Acta Archae-
ologica*, 34 (1963), 97–133.

[35] N. Egami and S. Masuda, *The Excavations at Tall-i-Bakun,
1956* (Tokyo, 1962).

[36] V. Masson, *Antiquity*, 35 (1961), 203–213.

pian shore.[37] In opening up the earliest traces of settled life in Anatolia, Turkish archaeologists received their most powerful aid from British excavators, notably Garstang at Mersin,[38] French at Can Hasan,[39] and Mellaart at Hacilar and Çatal Hüyük.[40]

In the case of India, archaeology was first developed by the occupying power. Interest stemmed, in part, from a concern for Sanskrit dating from the later eighteenth century and in part from the private activities of amateur archaeologists in the British community. Yet a predominant factor was official care. As long ago as 1861 Major-General Alexander Cunningham was appointed director-general of an archaeological survey of Northern India and during his twenty year tenure discovered, among other things, the site of Harappa. It is significant that one of Curzon's early acts as viceroy was to reconstitute the Archaeological Survey of India which he charged "to dig and to discover, to classify, reproduce and describe, and to cherish and conserve" the traces of ancient India. Ironically in this as in other respects he helped to fan sentiments that were to lead irresistibly to independence. As Michael Edwardes phrased it, "Curzon helped to build the edifice of national pride that was to support Indians in their struggle for India."[41] Curzon laid the foundations for the Services under which India and

[37] *Cave Excavations in Iran, 1949* (Philadelphia, 1951).
[38] *Prehistoric Mersin* (Oxford, 1953).
[39] *Anatolian Studies*, 12:27–40; 13:29–42; 14:125–134; 15:87–94.
[40] *Anatolian Studies*, 8:127–156; 9:51–66; 10:83–104; 11:39–76; *Çatal Hüyük: A Neolithic Town in Anatolia* (London, 1967).
[41] *History Today*, 12 (1962), 833–844.

Pakistan have carried forward archaeological research on their own account.

The relation of Europeans to the development of archaeology in China was very different. Since the seventeenth century, the educated classes in Western Europe had been charmed by Chinese taste; but it was not until the breakdown of the old regime that archaeologists from the outside world were able to work there. When they did come they entered a country in which archaeology had been cultivated for over two thousand years.[42] It is not surprising, therefore, that from the beginning they received active help from Chinese colleagues. If a Canadian, Davidson Black, was responsible for the first discovery of Pekin man and if Breuil and Teilhard de Chardin lent powerful assistance to the unveiling of the Old Stone Age in north China, it should be remembered that it was the Academia Sinica through its field director Pei Wen-Chung which systematically explored the most important locality at Choukoutien. Again, though a Swedish mining engineer, J. G. Anderson, was responsible for opening up the archaeology of settled communities in north China, the systematic excavation both of Neolithic settlements and graveyards and of An-yang and comparable sites of the Bronze Age was predominantly the work of the same institution.[43]

Western Europe also took the lead in opening up the study of early prehistory. The concept of transformism

[42] See note 6, p. 6.
[43] See J. G. Andersson, *Children of the Yellow Earth* (London, 1934); H. G. Creel, *The Birth of China* (London, 1936); William Watson, *China Before the Han Dynasty* (London, 1961).

and, in due course, the publication and widespread acceptance by educated people of a plausible hypothesis for the evolution of species—and by implication of man and his culture and institutions—were equally European. This in itself explains why research into the earlier phases of prehistory was at first concentrated on the Dordogne,[44] the European territory most richly furnished with easily recognizable sites for excavation. But there were other reasons why for two or three generations men were happy to concentrate on a territory so richly furnished and so conveniently close at hand. In the immediate post-Darwinian era, what seemed of prime and immediate importance was to fill the huge void opened up by the geological antiquity of man and recover as quickly as possible evidence of the evolution of his culture through the vicissitudes of the Ice Age. Again, however mistakenly as we may now think, many people tacitly accepted the notion of unilinear evolution as applied to man and his works.[45] In light of this, it was

[44] Edouard Lartet (d. 1871) began systematic work in the Dordogne in 1860. He was later joined by Henri Christy (d. 1865). Their joint work *Reliquiae Aquitanicae*, published in London in 1875, set a high standard for its time. Their excavations were followed by a large number undertaken by many prehistorians in the Dordogne and other parts of southwest France. The finds made during these years in this region provided the basis for the system devised by G. de Mortillet and revised by H. Breuil, a system that was improperly applied for a generation or two to material excavated from other regions.

[45] As recently as 1906 we find Gen. Pitt-Rivers, distinguished both as founder of the great collection at Oxford and as a pioneer of scientific field archaeology in Britain, expressing the view that "the existing races in their respective stages of progression may be

not merely convenient but also sensible to assemble the evidence for this process where it was plentiful and close at hand. By 1881 G. de Mortillet was ready in his *Musée préhistorique* to present a sequence (see Fig. 2) for the Old Stone Age which, modified by the Abbé Breuil in 1912,[46] provided a basic framework for the spate of volumes on prehistory that appeared in most of the principal European languages in the years 1911–1924.[47]

Yet such books could only present a stereotype of what really happened in prehistoric times. Before a genuine world prehistory could take shape, it was necessary for the techniques of research to be deployed far beyond the boundaries of Europe and, indeed, to the limits of the habitable world. Once again time does not allow of even the slightest sketch of the history of this process, yet it is still worth noting some of the leading factors involved. Expansionism was inherent in the subject, more especially on the part of those concerned with the remoter periods of prehistory. The scientific bent of many of them disposed them to adopt a world view impatient of fron-

---

taken as the bona fide representatives of the races of antiquity. . . . They thus afford us living illustrations of the social customs . . . which belong to the ancient races from which they remotely sprang." From J. L. Myres (ed.), *The Evolution of Culture and Other Essays* (Oxford, 1906), p. 53.

[46] "Les subdivisions du Paléolithique Supérieur et leur signification," *Compte rendu de la XIVᵉ Congrès international d'Anthropologie et d'Archéologie Préhistoriques* (Geneva, 1912; 2nd ed. 1937).

[47] E.g., H. Obermaier, *Der Mensch der Vorzeit* (Berlin, 1912); M. C. Burkitt, *Prehistory* (Cambridge, 1921); M. Boule, *Les Hommes Fossiles* (Paris, 1921); H. Obermaier, *Fossil Man in Spain* (New Haven, 1924).

TEMPS.			AGES.	PÉRIODES.	ÉPOQUES.
ACTUELS.	HISTORIQUES.		DU FER.	Mérovingienne.	WABENIENNE, Franque, Burgonde, Germanique.
				Romaine.	CHAMPDOLIENNE, Décadence Romaine.
					LUGDUNIENNE, Beau-temps Romain.
	PROTOHISTORIQUES.			Étrusque, Galatienne.	MARNIENNE, Gauloise, 3° Lacustre.
					HALLSTATTIENNE, des Tumulus, 1ro du Fer.
			DU BRONZE.	Bohémienne.	LARNAUDIENNE, 2° Lacustre en majeure partie.
					MORGIENNE, 2° Lacustre partie, des Dolmens partie.
GÉOLOGIQUES.	QUATERNAIRES.	PRÉHISTORIQUES.	DE LA PIERRE.	Néolithique, Pierre polie.	ROBENHAUSIENNE, 1re Lacustre, des Dolmens majeure partie. de l'Aurochs partie.
				Paléolithique, Pierre taillée.	MAGDALÉNIENNE, des Cavernes en majeure partie, du Renne en presque totalité.
					SOLUTRÉENNE, partie du Renne et du Mammouth.
					MOUSTÉRIENNE, du Mammouth majeure partie.
					CHELLÉENNE, Acheuléenne, du Grand Ours, de l'Éléphant antique.
	TERTIAIRES.			Éolithique, Pierre éclatée.	OTTAÏENNE, Tortonienne.
					THENAISIENNE, Aquitanienne.

FIG. 2. G. de Mortillet's chronological system (1881)

tiers or limitations. Again their habit of working forward in time made it natural for them to outflank and engulf the narrower territories marked out by those concerned with the genesis and impact of particular civilizations and incorporate all preliterate peoples wherever found within the *oecumene* of prehistory. Another factor that made for a world view was the involvement from a very early stage with ethnology.[48] In the early days of archaeology, accounts of travellers, missionaries, and traders from remote parts of the world brought home to Europeans better than anything else the fact that men could indeed exist beyond the bounds described by recorded history. Again, given the misconception prevalent in the Darwinian aftermath that the preliterate peoples of the day could be taken as representatives of stages of culture through which civilized man has passed in the course of prehistoric ages,[49] it is not difficult to see why European prehistorians of the earlier periods were receptive to discoveries made overseas.

Also, archaeology formed part of the cultural equipment carried by Europeans to the extensive territories they colonised on other continents. As settled life developed and wealth and leisure increased, it was only to be expected that archaeology should have been pursued alongside other hobbies and avocations in the new homelands. In fact we know that pioneers like J. L. Stephens in America,[50] Thomas Bowker in South Africa,[51] and

[48] Already in 1865 Sir John Lubbock devoted three chapters of his *Pre-historic Times* to modern savages.

[49] See note 45, p. 25.

[50] John Lloyd Stephens was a New York lawyer who first explored the monuments of Yucatan taking as his companion an architect, Frederick Catherwood, whose illustrations greatly enriched the two-volume *Incidents of Travel in Central America, Chiapas and Yucatan* (New York, 1841).

[51] Thomas Holden Bowker's family came to the Albany district

28

Bruce Foote in India[52] were able to stake out new territories for archaeology and that in due time museums, universities, and other learned bodies institutionalised and organised this field of enquiry. Even colonial governments, it may no longer be so unfashionable to admit, played an important part in this respect. We have already seen how the British in India provided for the care of ancient monuments and even supported archaeological research on a considerable scale (see p. 23). No less remarkable were the services to archaeology rendered by the French in Indo-China and the Dutch in Indonesia. In the field of prehistoric archaeology the most outstanding contributions were perhaps those made in different parts of Africa. In French North Africa, work of outstanding quality was achieved by the Services des antiquités et des monuments historiques in both Algeria and Morocco.[53] In Belgium, the Musée royal de

---

of Cape Province in the 1820s. He collected flint implements of the South African Middle Stone Age in 1858, the year before Prestwich and Evans visited Abbeville and accepted the tools found by Boucher de Perthes in the Somme Valley gravels. Some of Bowker's finds are still in the Grahamstown Museum. See J. Desmond Clark, *The Prehistory of Southern Africa* (London, 1959), pp. 24–25.

[52] Robert Bruce Foote discovered the first Paleolithic tools in the laterite deposits near Madras in 1863. In 1872 he visited one of the Deccan Neolithic ash mounds; his conclusion that they consisted of fired cow dung was overlaid by nearly three generations of more or less absurd conjecture until vindicated by scientific analysis in 1953. In their recent book *The Birth of Indian Civilization* (London, 1968), Bridget and Raymond Allchin wrote of Foote, "In 1949 it was still possible to say that almost every important site in peninsular India owed its discovery to him" (p. 21).

[53] See, for example, M. L. Balout's *Préhistoire de l'afrique du*

l'afrique at Tervuren acted as the main center for archaeological research in the Belgian Congo.[54] In the former British colonies in different parts of Africa, such archaeological research as flourished was locally based. In at least one case it was supported consciously as a way of helping the people to acquire and build up a sense of national identity. In Nigeria, the Antiquities Service was set up in 1943, and in 1952 the Museum at Jos was opened to display the numerous antiquities including significant works of art salvaged from the tin-workings over the years. In introducing the second reading of the First Antiquities Ordinance in 1953, the minister of works, the Hon. Abubakar Tafawa Balewa pointed out that unlike many things brought into the country "our antiquities and traditional arts are Nigerian" and went on to state in so many words that, "owing to the absence of written records, the old arts of Nigeria represent a large part of the evidence of our history."[55] In the northeast of the continent, notable work was accomplished by the Sudan Antiquities Service established under the colonial administration, notably in the term of office of Commissioner A. J. Arkell.[56] Further south, in Kenya

---

nord (Paris, 1955) or M. P. Biberson's Monographs published as Fascicules 16 and 17 of the *Publications du Service des Antiquités du Maroc* (Rabat, 1961).

[54] E.g., Jacques Nenquin's *Contribution to the Study of the Prehistoric Cultures of Rwanda and Barundi* (Tervuren, 1967).

[55] See the booklet *Preserving the Past* issued in 1959 by the Federal Ministry of Research and Information, Lagos.

[56] See Arkell's books, *The Old Stone Age in the Anglo-Egyptian Sudan* (Khartoum, 1949); *Early Khartoum* (Oxford, 1949); and *Shaheinab* (Oxford, 1953).

and adjacent territories, Louis and Mary Leakey have shown East Africa to be perhaps the most important province of the Lower Paleolithic world.[57] Again, under Dr. Desmond Clark's direction, the Rhodes Livingstone Museum became a key centre of prehistoric research during the closing phase of the colonial era; nor in considering the contribution made by men of European origins to African prehistory should one overlook the massive contributions made by the former colony of Southern Rhodesia or by the Union of South Africa.[58]

Striking testimony to the sound foundations laid by the leading colonial powers is that the archaeological institutions they created have been retained and developed by the newly emergent nations. This does not alter that fact that it was the dissolution of the colonial system that more than anything else stimulated the growth of archaeological research in much of Africa and Asia. The new nations experienced the same passion to project their identities backward in time as their former masters had done, both in their own homelands and in the territories that cradled the ancient civilizations from which their own had profited. Despite shortages of money and trained men, the new countries have eagerly pressed on with archaeological research.[59] Thus, European imperialism

[57] See L. S. B. Leakey, *Olduvai Gorge* (Cambridge, 1951) and *Olduvai Gorge, 1951–1961* (Cambridge, 1965); M. D. Leakey in *Background to Evolution in Africa*, eds. W. W. Bishop and J. D. Clark (Chicago, 1967), pp. 417–442; and Sonia Coles, *The Prehistory of East Africa* (London, 1954).

[58] The best summary is provided by J. Desmond Clark's *The Prehistory of Southern Africa* (London, 1959), pp. 24 ff.

[59] A good way of gauging the vitality of prehistoric archaeology

31

and the reaction of indigenous peoples have both served to further expansion of knowledge and awareness of the prehistoric past. As the peoples of the whole world became incorporated within the nexus of the civilization and technology first developed in Europe and as they followed the model of nationhood that after all first emerged in that continent, they were at the same time drawn inexorably within the *oecumene* of world prehistory.

This applied no less to the states of eastern Europe formally dedicated to the materialist interpretation of history, all of which, including imperial Russia, had shared in the national pursuit of archaeology before being overtaken by communism. The programmes administered by the Institutes for the History of Material Culture, both in the Soviet Union and in its satellites, have indeed been massive.[60] Although technically and ideo-

---

in India since independence is to consult the summary of proceedings of the seminar on Indian prehistory and proto-history held to mark the centenary of Deccan College and published under the title *Indian Prehistory, 1964*, ed. V. M. Misra and M. S. Mate (Poona, 1965). Of forty delegates some thirty-nine held posts in India; these included eleven members of the Indian Archaeological Survey, members of three state archaeological services, and representatives of no less than eleven universities as well as of the National Museum at Delhi and of several research institutes.

[60] For some insight into the achievements of Soviet archaeology, see A. L. Mongait, *Archaeology in the U.S.S.R.*, trans. M. W. Thompson (London, 1961). In the east European states of Bulgaria, Czechoslovakia, Hungary, Poland, Rumania, and Yugoslavia, prehistoric archaeology is conducted mainly under the aegis of institutes grouped under their respective academies. A good insight into activities in one of these countries, Czechoslo-

logically disappointing in the sense that they have failed to enlarge notably the capabilities of the subject, they have nevertheless extended and made more precise our knowledge of extensive tracts of eastern Europe and Siberia. The ideological drive of communism has thus worked in the same direction as the other forces already mentioned.

A decisive turning point came between the two world wars. It was reached, as Dorothy Garrod explained[61] in her now classic address "The Upper Paleolithic in the Light of Recent Discovery," as a result of "the multiplication of researches outside Europe. Excavations in Africa, the Near East, Asiatic Russia and China [she wrote in 1948] have opened up a new field for speculation, and at the same time have revealed the unsuspected complexity of many problems which to de Mortillet and other pioneers seemed relatively simple." The shift from a Europocentric to a truly worldwide conception of prehistory was symbolised by the African and Far Eastern travels and researches of the Abbé Breuil,[62] the nearest approach to a pontif the subject is likely to possess. Miss

---

vakia, can be won from the well-illustrated monthly periodical, *Archaeologické rozhledy* or, again, from the summary *Investigations archéologiques en Tchécoslovakie* prepared for the VIIth International Congress of Pre- and Proto-historic Sciences held in Prague in 1966. Although the ruling Communist party maintains a close grip on scientific activity through the academies, it is not difficult to detect strong nationalist drives behind the archaeological activities of these states.

[61] *Proceedings of the Prehistoric Society*, 4 (1938), 1–26.

[62] See *Miscelanea en Homenaje al Abate Henri Breuil* (Barcelona, 1965), 2:141–143, 251–269.

Garrod was surely right to acknowledge his example, yet
we may suspect that at most the abbé speeded up, if he
did not merely signal, a development that was in any case
on the way.

What is at least sure is that when prehistoric research
was able to resume after World War II, the objective was
no longer in doubt. In addition to the task of furthering
indigenous archaeology, long undertaken by older states
and eagerly adopted by the new, the nineteenth-century
idea of traversing frontiers in pursuit of archaeology has
been expanded from the territories of prime interest
to Europeans to the whole world, an achievement far
more difficult to realise in practice than during the period of Western hegemony. The continuing efforts of European states in this field have already been touched
on (pp. 26–31). It remains to emphasise the particularly
notable contributions made by the United States of
America operating through universities, museums, and
other foundations concerned with research and with
good relations between states. To mention only a few,
one is entitled here to begin by recalling the expeditions
sent out over the years from the University of California
at Berkeley to Africa, Mesoamerica, and Peru.[63] As other
examples, one might quote the long series of campaigns
mounted in Southwest Asia by the Oriental Institute of
Chicago,[64] the assaults on Troy and Pylos by the Univer-

[63] Notably, the work of Drs. Desmond Clark, Robert Heizer, and
J. H. Rowe.

[64] One need only refer to the researches published in the mono-
graph series *Studies in Ancient Oriental Civilization* or to such
names as J. H. Breasted, Henri Frankfort, or Robert Braidwood
to make the point.

The Relevance of World Prehistory

sity of Cincinatti,[65] Harvard's long record of research in Mesoamerica and western Europe,[66] the University Museum of Pennsylvania's well-judged coverage of almost every part of the world,[67] and not least the discriminating aid accorded by the Wenner-Gren Foundation of New York[68] to international prehistory and the still more re-

[65] Excavation at Troy was resumed (1932–1938) by Dr. Carl Blegen who has also edited the full report *Troy* (4 vols.) for the Princeton University Press (1950–1958). Only interim reports have yet appeared on the Pylos excavations.

[66] The *Memoirs* and to some extent the *Papers, of the Peabody Museum of American Archaeology and Ethnology, Harvard University* reflect a strong preoccupation with Maya civilization, but powerful contributions have also been made to European prehistory. Among these are the series of monographs published in the *Bulletin of the American School of Prehistoric Research*, founded in 1921 by Dr. Grant MacCurdy and directed by him until 1945, when Dr. Hugh Hencken took over the task. Among important excavations directed from Harvard in Europe have been those undertaken by the Harvard Archaeological Expedition in Ireland (1932–1936) and Dr. Hallam Movius' work at the Abri Pataud in the Dordogne, backed by the National Science Foundation.

[67] The University Museum of the University of Pennsylvania operates a research program which imaginatively covers the world, as well as making key contributions to the development of scientific aids to archaeology. For a general impression, see the museum's bulletin *Expedition*.

[68] The Wenner-Gren Foundation for Anthropological Research, founded as the Viking Fund in 1941, was launched on a new phase in its career at the International Symposium on Anthropology held in 1952 at New York under the chairmanship of Dr. A. L. Kroeber. See *Anthropology Today: An Encyclopaedic Inventory* (Chicago: University of Chicago Press, 1953). The foundation furthers the whole range of anthropological research and has given most discriminating aid to prehistory, both through the

35

cent initiative of the Ford Foundation toward the training of young American archaeologists who wish to work overseas. Even more encouraging, in some respects, have been the initiatives of UNESCO, both in furthering the publication of the fruits of international research[69] and, above all perhaps, in securing the cooperation of scholars and institutions of many nations in such practical projects as the salvage of Nubian archaeology threatened by the construction of the Aswan Dam, a project in which expeditions from both sides of the Iron Curtain cooperated fruitfully with one from the New World.[70] Increases in the range and depth of research have been reflected in the multiplication of international and

---

symposia held at Burg Wartenstein (see, for example, *Background to Evolution in Africa*, ed. W. H. Bishop and J. Desmond Clark, Chicago, 1967) and by means of grants to carefully chosen projects.

[69] For example, through the *Journal of World History*, which made available summaries of particular fields by eminent specialists, and through the synthesis by Jacquetta Hawkes and Sir Leonard Woolley in their *Prehistory and the Beginning of Civilization* (London, 1963).

[70] For example, the Nubian expedition sponsored jointly by Columbia and Southern Methodist (Dallas) universities, together with the Museum of New Mexico, had joint participation from other institutions in America, Belgium, France, Egypt, and Poland and enjoyed financial support from the U.S. State Department and the Smithsonian Institution. See Fred. Wendorf, *The Prehistory of Nubia*, 3 vols. (Dallas, Texas, 1968). Again, the series of expeditions mounted by Yale (1962–1965) involved the cooperation of scholars and scientists from several other universities and received financial backing from the National Science Foundation, the U.S. State Department, and a number of university institutions. See Foreword to Karl W. Butzer and Carl L. Hansen, *Desert and River in Nubia* (Madison: University of Wisconsin Press, 1968).

The Relevance of World Prehistory

broadly regional congresses,[71] as well as in the proliferation of learned monographs and periodicals. At the same time, popular interest has led to the production of an ever expanding number of popular illustrated books on archaeology as well as features on radio and television, the cumulative effect of which has been to create a climate of opinion favourable to archaeological projects which in themselves inevitably grow more expensive with every application of technology and science.

Successive applications of techniques originally developed in fields as diverse as oil prospection and military reconnaissance have greatly eased and made more exhaustive the task of archaeological discovery, and the

[71] The original series of International Congresses of Anthropology and Prehistoric Archaeology covered the whole field of anthropology and met exclusively in Europe (from Spezia in 1865 to Portugal in 1930). When the congress was in effect split into two, archaeology fell largely to the Congress of Pre- and Protohistoric Sciences, which has continued to confine its meetings to Europe (London, 1932; Oslo, 1936; Zürich, 1950; Madrid, 1954; Hamburg, 1958; Rome, 1962; Prague, 1966). On the other hand, some fields of prehistoric research, more especially those outside the province of Old World civilization, have been catered for by the parallel Congress of Anthropological and Ethnological Sciences, which has managed to break out of Europe as a place of meeting (London, 1934; Copenhagen, 1938; Brussels, 1948; Vienna, 1952; Philadelphia, 1956; Paris, 1960; Moscow, 1964; Tokyo-Kyoto, 1968). Separate provision for New World archaeology is of long-standing duration. A feature of the period since the Second World War has been the rise of conferences confined to major regions outside Europe. One of the most significant of these is the Pan-African Conference on Prehistory (Nairobi, 1947; Algiers, 1952; Livingstone, 1955; Leopoldville, 1959; Tenerife, 1963; and Dakar, 1967).

37

various sciences have transformed the possibilities of extracting information from the primary data recovered by excavation.[72] To take a single example, one can hardly overstress the relevance to international prehistory of the radiocarbon dating method developed by the nuclear physicist, Willard Libby.[73] This single addition to the armoury of prehistoric studies has contributed more than any other single factor to complete the world coverage of prehistoric archaeology, not to mention the way it has helped scholars to synchronise phenomena in different parts of the world. The worldwide application of radiocarbon dating has been greatly helped by the erection of a network of laboratories not only in western Europe and North America, but also in the Soviet Union, Japan, Australia, and New Zealand—in itself an apt illustration of the unifying effect of modern science. As examples of the way in which radiocarbon dating has accelerated research, one can appreciate, first, how rapidly the earliest settlement of the New World (Fig. 3) has been reconstructed considering that the original site at Folsom was not discovered until 1926;[74] second, how within the last five or ten years radiocarbon dating has put Australia firmly into the picture of world prehistory, even though the first stratigraphic excavation in that country was not

[72] For a useful summary see Don Brothwell and Eric Higgs (eds.), *Science and Aarchaeology* (London, 1969).

[73] W. F. Libby, *Radiocarbon Dating*, 2nd ed. (Chicago, 1955).

[74] J. D. Figgins and H. J. Cook, *Natural History*, 27 (1927), 229–247. The rapidity with which the Paleoindian phase of New World prehistory was recovered can be guaged from successive editions of Marie Wormington's *Ancient Man in North America* (Denver: 1st ed., 1939; 4th ed., 1957).

The Relevance of World Prehistory

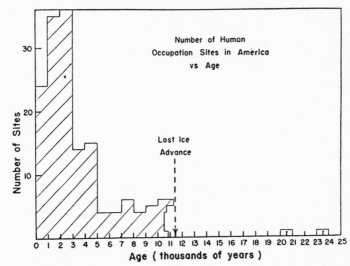

FIG. 3. Radiocarbon dating of early human settlement in the New World *(after Vance Haynes)*

undertaken and recorded until 1929;[75] and third, how breathtaking has been the speed with which the Japanese have been able to reveal the succession of early lithic and Jomon stages.[76]

[75] H. M. Hale and N. B. Tindale, *Records of the South Australian Museum*, 4 (1930), 145–218. For an account of the history of early prehistoric investigation in Australia, see J. D. Mulvaney in *Proceedings of the Prehistoric Society*, 27 (1961), 56–107. For a summary of results down to 1967, see the present author's *World Prehistory: A New Outline* (Cambridge, 1969), chap. 11.

[76] The most useful paper (Japanese text, but table and illustrations) on early lithic finds with C-14 dates is Chosuke Serizawa's "The Chronology of Palaeolithic Industries and Carbon 14 Dates in Japan," *Reports of the Research Institute for Japanese Culture*, no. 3. (Sendai, Japan: Tohoku University, 1967). For a full list of Jomon C-14 dates, see J. E. Kidder, *Prehistoric Japanese Arts: Jomon Pottery* (Tokyo, Japan, and Palo Alto, California, 1968), p. 268 and table.

39

The main outlines are already on the canvas and many practised hands are filling in the details of the picture of mankind's prehistory. I have used the analogy of a canvas. I should, of course, have spoken of a film, a film full of motion and traversing not only space but time, the lifespans of thousands and indeed tens of thousands of generations of men. What is the significance of this film? This is a question to which educators at every level might well address themselves as they seek to inform and educate the more intelligent minority whose role it is to give direction and stability as well as specialised services to society.

At the risk of being thought reactionary—and there are contexts in which even this can be faced with equanimity —one might suggest that there is still room even in higher education for the inculcation of values and even of ideals, provided these are grounded in humanity. If the academic study of prehistory can go any way toward enlarging and amplifying the range and quality of historical awareness, to make it easier for men of diverse cultural backgrounds to live together in amity without sacrificing their unique qualities, then it more than justifies its place in the curriculum of any university. Expressed in a sentence, the significance of world prehistory is the contribution it is able to make to widening the perspectives of history in accord with the needs of today.

It is surely no coincidence that this concept should have taken shape when the world is, despite all its political rivalries, being drawn inexorably into the ambit of a single world market; when technology is so greatly reducing the size of the world so far as the communication of news is concerned; and above all when universalising scientific modes of thought are sweeping through all the various civilizations of men. By and large, it is reasonable to assume that men have the kind of history that best accords with prevailing conditions of social life. Some concern with the past is basic to humanity itself in the sense that human groups are so constituted by virtue of inheriting specific traditions. The traditional lore shared by the members of particular societies served not only to heighten their sense of solidarity, but also to differentiate them from others in much the same way as do differences in plumage or song among birds.

Under the conditions that prevailed universally throughout nearly the whole of human history, and which still obtain today among the few peoples living outside or at least on the remoter margins of civilization, the areas of territorial and historical awareness alike were narrowly restricted. People knew intimately the areas over which they moved in the course of the quest for food, and they might have some more generalised knowledge of the remoter territories from which they drew supplies by means of one form of exchange or another; but of the great world outside they had no glimmer of knowledge. The same was true of historical awareness. The stories conveyed by the elders at the initiation ceremonies, in the course of which young men were admitted as members of adult society, have habitually been concerned first and foremost with the way in which the ancestors laid down the customs of the tribe and even shaped the features of the familiar landscape.[77] As history they were strictly limited in range, but they served the

[77] E.g., the Alchera myths of the Arunta. See Sir Baldwin Spencer *Wanderings in Wild Australia* (London, 1928), vol. 1, chap. 2.

essential purpose of enhancing group solidarity and validating the social institutions and even the environment of the tribe. In other words, the area of geographical and historical awareness was adapted fairly narrowly to circumstances; people were aware of what it was necessary for them to be aware. Conversely, the larger a community became, the wider the territory occupied by people sharing the same culture and the more extensive the area of historical awareness.

Concurrently, the more complex a society became, the more intricate became its history. As we know from the Homeric poems, the Rig-Veda, and the epics of the Celtic and Teutonic peoples, it was possible to transmit lengthy and detailed narratives by word of mouth. Yet the time came when it became convenient to write histories down; and for all peoples with a recorded literature it is possible to obtain a close insight into the extent of their historical awareness.[78] In every case, awareness extended no further than the range of interest of the people concerned; within this range a basic distinction was made between "we" and "they," between the civilized and the barbarian.[79] Where ancient maps exist they reflect in a graphic manner the range of territorial concern. In the case of inland peoples like the Babylonians,

[78] This is dramatically illustrated by the distinctive scripts in which the earliest historical records were written down. There is no need to read an inscription to tell whose history is being recorded; one has merely to identify the script. See David Diringer, *The Alphabet: A Key to the History of Mankind* (London, 1948); *Writing* (London, 1962).

[79] This is seen very well in the Emperor Ch'ien Lung's attitude to Lord Macartney as envoy of George III. In accepting the diplo-

this might be restricted more or less narrowly to the home territories and their frontiers. Again, the Chinese, although at different periods conducting trade with the West by way of Inner Asia and drawing wealth from maritime commerce with the Philippines, Indonesia, and Southeast Asia, not to mention contacts with Arab traders in the ports of South India and Ceylon, were basically landlocked and xenophobic.[80] With seafaring peoples, on the other hand, geographical knowledge was often much more wide-ranging; for instance, the Classical Greeks sailed over the whole Mediterranean and around the Atlantic shores of Europe, the Black and Red seas, the Persian Gulf, and India, a territory only peripherally enlarged by the Romans (see Fig. 4). All the early civilized peoples, though drawing wealth to a varying extent from trade or even colonisation, were at bottom interested in themselves and equated history with their own doings. The fact that the expansion of European dominion overseas, following the great age of maritime discovery, was largely predatory calls for no remark; what is more revealing is the element of idealism. Certainly the Europeans wanted gold and spices, but they also sought with varying degrees of zeal to impose their

---

matic gifts as a form of tribute to his "Dynasty's majestic virtue," the emperor felt constrained to emphasize how little value he attached to them in themselves: "Our Celestial Empire possesses all things in prolific abundance and lacks no product within its border. We do not need to import the manufactures of outside barbarians in exchange for our own produce." Sir John T. Pratt, *China and Britain* (London, n.d.), p. 49.

[80] Sir A. F. Whyte, *China and Foreign Powers* (London, 1927), p. 41.

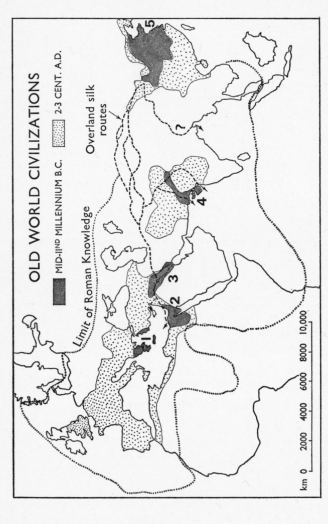

OLD WORLD CIVILIZATIONS

MID-IIND MILLENNIUM B.C.

2-3 CENT. A.D.

Limit of Roman Knowledge

Overland silk routes

km 0   2000 4000 6000 8000 10,000

FIG. 4. Old World civilizations in the mid-second millennium B.C. and the second and third centuries A.D. (*after Bengtson, Milojčić, and others*). 1. Mycenaean Greece; 2. Egypt (Hyksos); 3. Babylonia (Hammurabi); 4. Indian (Harappan); 5. Chinese (Shang).

own religion, customs, and even political systems on who-
ever could be made to accept them. The concept of the
white man's burden grew out of his belief that he was a
superior person. His mission was to convert the heathen,
or at least to teach them how to play cricket. He wanted
to make other men behave as he did.

Perhaps it is not surprising that at Cambridge thirty
years ago, Ancient History was equated with the history
of the Biblical and Classical peoples, that Medieval History was identified with the history of the rise of Chris-
tendom, or that Modern History should still have been
interpreted as the history of European states and their
overseas dependencies. History, as taught in Europe, was
unabashedly Europocentric, just as that of Classical
Greece was Hellenic and that of China Sinocentric. The
anomaly only became apparent when European dominion was spread over other lands—some of them the homes
of civilizations of even greater antiquity—or, perhaps one
ought rather to say, when European hegemony was re-
pudiated by newly emergent states all over the world.

In the meantime, before the power shift at the close of
the Second World War had brought down the overseas
empires of the great Western powers, historians of pro-
phetic type had already exposed the pretensions of Europocentric history, notably Oswald Spengler writing at the
end of the First and Arnold Toynbee during the run up
to the Second World War. Both have been severely attacked by professional historians for their propensity
to mould history into overall patterns of a pseudo-
philosophical order. Yet, each in his own way contributed to opening up the scope of history. Spengler derided

a system under which "The ground of West Europe is treated as a steady pole, a unique patch of the sphere for no better reason, it seems, than because we live on it— and great histories of millennial duration, and mighty far-away Cultures are made to revolve around this pole in all modesty. It is a quaintly conceived system of sun and planets!" And he went on to claim to have replaced what he terms a Ptolemaic system of history, in which other civilizations were held to follow orbits around us, by a Copernican one that "admits of no sort of privileged position to the Classical or Western Culture as against the Cultures of India, Babylon, China, Egypt, the Arabs, Mexico—separate worlds of dynamic being which in point of mass count for just as much in the general picture of history as the Classical, while frequently surpassing it in point of spiritual greatness and soaring power."[81]

The apocalyptic[82] and plangent tone of Spengler's writings, combined with the fact that they issued from a country whose regime was plunging into a trough of disaster that many considered well merited, combined to diminish their direct impact on the English-speaking world. Yet, in a vital respect, the message of Arnold Toynbee's *A Study of History*[83] was essentially the same,

[81] Oswald Spengler's *Untergang der Abendlandes* was published in two volumes (1918–1922) and appeared in English (trans. C. F. Atkinson) in 1926–1929. The passages are quoted from Atkinson's translation, vol. 1, pp. 17–18.

[82] Cf. Sir Herbert Butterfield's perceptive remark in *Man on His Past* (Cambridge, 1955): "Indeed, the belief that civilization must collapse unless one's own state or empire prevails in international affairs is probably common to all great political organisms" (p. 118).

[83] Published in six volumes (1934–1939) and summarized in D. C. Somervell's *Abridgement* (Oxford, 1946).

even if his writing was more scholarly and temperate. We should never, he warned, allow the economic and political power of Europe in the world of his time to obscure the fact that Western Civilization was only one of the many that once existed and of several even now existing in the world.

It is the fate of prophets to be overtaken by events, and no one today needs to be reminded of the relativity of the European view of history. What we need now, surely, is a broadly anthropological view of history, one that can reconcile the experience of the several great literate civilizations with that of communities until a few generations ago prehistoric. As Professor Herbert Muller has written in his *Uses of the Past*, "It is a commonplace that we must establish some kind of world order, and we cannot hope to do so without breadth of understanding and sympathy. Our scientific, aesthetic, moral, and urgently practical interests alike call out . . . [for] an anthropological view of our own history, an effort to see in perspective not only our nation but our civilization."[84]

How is this to be achieved? How are we in the context of today to gain a genuinely world view of history? Surely it will be by viewing all the several literate, history-recording civilizations of men as outgrowths from a common trunk rooted in prehistoric antiquity. Only so can we understand the truly cousinly relationship of all civilizations and only so can we appreciate at their proper worth as independent experiments in social living, the contributions made by societies that were still preliterate when first incorporated within the community of mod-

[84] Oxford, 1952. Quoted from the Mentor Book edition (New York, 1954), p. 441.

ern nations. To express the matter another way, one could say that a view of history adequate to modern times can only be had by taking account of the whole of man's life on earth and remembering that almost all of this has, in fact, been prehistoric. Arnold Toynbee showed some signs of recognising this when he wrote that the "mutation of sub-man into man, which was accomplished in circumstances of which we have no record, under the aegis of primitive societies, was a more profound change, a greater step in growth, than any progress which man has yet achieved under the aegis of civilization."[85] He was prevented from grasping the possibilities of world prehistory by some lack of sympathy with the archaeological method, as well, no doubt, as by the immense gaps that still existed in our knowledge when he wrote, a generation and a half ago.

Today we are in a more fortunate position; for the first time we can each view our histories in relation to other histories as well as to the vast preliterate ages of man. What does this imply? Do we have to fit ourselves for the one world of science and technology by wholesale abandonment of our traditional histories or lore? Or, have we to learn in all their detail the intricate histories of all peoples? We have surely to do none of these things. Quite plainly it is impossible to study and teach the history of all peoples without losing the particularity and detail that are the special merit of history. The answer can only be for us each to study our own history,[86] the

[85] *Abridgement,* p. 49.

[86] Cf. Prof. G. Elton's *The Future of the Past: An Inaugural Lecture* (Cambridge, 1968).

history of our own group in the context of our own civilization, our own civilization in the context of other civilizations, and all civilizations in the context of world prehistory.

It is wrong to imagine that we would any of us be better off if we could shed our own history and culture and conform along with all other peoples to the generalised or homogenised pattern we recognise in the concourse areas of airports the world over. We do not have to become bored to death in order to live together; we merely have to be tolerant. And tolerance does not mean a lack of regard for our own culture, our own history, but on the contrary a positive regard for all cultures and all histories. Men are men by virtue of sharing cultural traditions, not any job lot of traditions but the traditions of the particular groups in which they were born and brought up. The idea that, because cultural chauvinism is reprehensible, culture itself is something to be ashamed of is like the argument that because patriotism is abused it ought to be abolished. The fallacy is to assume that a man lacking in cultural commitment and deficient in patriotic feeling is likely to make a better citizen of the world by virtue of these negative attributes. It is distressing for an anthropologist to hear behaviour praised for being "natural." Of course there is a sense in which human behaviour can hardly be anything else, but in the sense to which I refer it is used to contrast with "cultural": "natural" behaviour is opposed approvingly to "artificial" behaviour. This is an abominable doctrine. Human values, and by definition behaviour conditioned by these values, cannot be "natural" in this

49

sense; they can only be artificial, the product not merely of human society but of the history of particular human societies. Man is, of course, an animal; but he is a peculiar kind of animal or at least he is in so far as his behaviour is patterned by culture, by the culture he shares by virtue of belonging to particular societies. Human values, that is the values that constitute men, are artificial, the product of specific cultural traditions—in particular historical contexts. Men can only enrich mankind by contributing the insights of their own particular cultures. To divest oneself of culture is thus to lose one's very humanity; one cannot remain human while eschewing the historic traditions, the inheritance of which alone constitutes humanity. What we need, then, is anything but cultural nudity. On the contrary, we have to cultivate a reverence for the usages, history, and traditions of all peoples including our own—and not merely of all living peoples, but of all peoples who have ever lived.

Some, admittedly, became civilized before others. But what of this? World prehistory makes it sufficiently plain that both literacy and urban living are extremely recent. From the perspective allowed by prehistory we are all on much the same level. All peoples alike, whatever their experiences during the last couple of hundred generations, have shared a common process of hominization extending over perhaps the previous hundred thousand. This makes it easier to understand, among other things, how it is that peoples who were prehistoric down to the nineteenth century have been able to acquire the arts and manners of civilization so quickly. Some of the newer nations have had their troubles; but when we consider their recent history, the most striking thing about them is surely their success in running their own affairs and sharing, as far as their means allow, in modern institutions and technology. Despite every setback, the conditions necessary for the emergence of a world community are already in the process of taking shape and with them the need for new historical perspectives, the kind of perspectives that only prehistory makes possible. Our survival depends on, among other things, our ability to view one another in a historical context appropriate to a world that shrinks in size and grows in potential danger with every passing year. History is emphatically not over and done with—at least we hope it is not. It is something which to a large degree determines how we behave. Let us view all histories and all prehistory in a world perspective; in honouring the achievements of our own and of all other peoples, we are after all acknowledging our own humanity.

Prehistory is not something human beings lived through long ago. It is with us still. A bare couple of hundred generations ago all peoples were prehistoric. And we would do well to remember that a sizable number of the states now constituting the United Nations were prehistoric down to modern times. Even in its present state of imperfection, prehistory is capable of helping men to understand and, therefore, to participate more effectively in the modern world. Yet we might well remember how much remains to be discovered and understood. Vast territories remain to be explored and many problems have hardly yet been broached. I, for one, am confident that the tremendous efforts now being made and to be made all over the world by the combined efforts of prehistoric archaeologists, cultural anthropologists, and a broad range of natural scientists will yield an ever richer harvest in human well-being as well as in that depth of understanding which is as necessary to civilized man as bread itself.

2

Material Progress

Man may be excused for feeling some pride at having risen, though not through his own exertions, to the very summit of the organic scale.

CHARLES DARWIN

(*From the closing paragraph of* The Descent of Man, *1871.*)

OR OVER A HUNDRED YEARS it has hardly been possible to doubt that as an organism man has emerged in the course of biological evolution through the same process of natural selection responsible for the appearance of other animals. There is no significant break in the paleontological record. Man is merely the most recent genus to have appeared.[87] Zoologically speaking, he is not to be separated from forms of life that emerged many hundreds of millions of years ago. Yet beyond doubt he is the most successful animal. He has not merely multiplied in numbers, occupied the widest range of habitats, and learned to manipulate and use a vast range of animals and plants; he has also entered a new dimension of life through a massive development in his sense of self-awareness.

Here my concern is first and foremost with the material basis of this new form of life—that is, with what is frequently termed man's material culture, the means by which he has supplemented his limbs and muscles in satisfying his organic needs. It is, after all, by the use of artifacts that man has been able to extend the use of his environment and enter on a course of expanding horizons. Yet it is important to remember that in possessing cultural attributes man is by no means unique; many

[87] For a succinct and authoritative statement, see Sir Wilfrid Le Gros Clark's *The Fossil Evidence for Human Evolution*, 2nd ed. (Chicago, 1964).

other organisms, some of them of quite lowly status from an evolutionary point of view, use extraneous objects to further their ends and acquire some other aspects of their behaviour by virtue of belonging to particular groups.[88] It is hardly possible, therefore, to separate man from other animals solely on the basis of his possession of culture. Where he differs rather is in the degree to which he has come to depend on this.

The physical evolution of man is relevant to our theme only in so far as this made possible and at the same time was itself conditioned by cultural development. In the fossil record some animals, once highly successful and even dominant in their day, failed to survive changes in their environment.[89] The very completeness of their organic adaptation to particular sets of conditions meant that when these changed they were unable to compete with animals better adapted to and, therefore, selected for survival in the new environment. If man avoided the fate of the dinosaurs and mastodons, he did so essentially because he remained relatively unspecialised as an organism. To a slight degree, it is true, he adapted to environmental conditions through his physique, notably pigmentation[90] and width of nasal aperture;[91] but in the main he adapted to changing circumstances through his

[88] See under note 96, p. 64.

[89] Julian Huxley makes the point well in his essay, "The Evolutionary Process," in *Evolution as a Process*, ed. Julian Huxley *et al.* (London, 1954), p. 11.

[90] Thus, the amount of pigment in the outer layer of a dark skin has been held to protect a man from harmful ultraviolet rays of the sun, whereas a pale skin is advantageous in a temperate climate, because it allows the sun to activate the synthesis of vitamin

culture, a medium capable of far more rapid and perfect adjustment to the most varying conditions.

In retrospect one can see how man's biological evolution prepared him for and also made possible his cultural evolution and equally how his cultural evolution has allowed him to remain physically unspecialised.[92] The two processes unfolded side by side and interacted one upon the other. The most important and decisive biological change reflected in the fossils was the adoption of a habitually upright stance, since until the hands were freed from the task of locomotion they were not so readily available for manipulating objects and ultimately making the tools and weapons by which the aims of the organism could be more effectively realised. This morphological change may well be related to the fact that, in contrast to the great apes who lived in a forest environment and continued to rely to a considerable degree on the forelimbs for getting about, the immediate ancestors of man were apparently adapted to life in the open where the need to cope with other animals placed a premium on freeing the hands. As fossils of the australopithecines

---

D. See Bernard Campbell, *Human Evolution: An Introduction to Man's Adaptations* (London, 1967), p. 243.

[91] The degree of correlation between the width of nasal aperture and climate was demonstrated by A. Thomson and L. H. D. Buxton in their classic paper "Man's Nasal Index in Relation to Certain Climatic Conditions," in *Journal of the Royal Anthropological Institute*, 53 (1923).

[92] For the feedback between biology and social behaviour in human evolution, see S. L. Washburn, "Behaviour and the Origin of Man," *Journal of the Royal Anthropological Institute*, 97 (1967), 21–27.

suggest, an upright stance was adopted while the brain was still of the same order of magnitude as that of the great apes.[93] The enlargement of the brain (see Fig. 5) that helped to define the earliest men may well have been assisted by or even have resulted from the stimulus that came from the greatly increased use, and in due course the manufacture, of tools and weapons. Conversely, it was the brain, working in conjunction with the hands,[94] that shaped the cultural apparatus by which man has won his dominance; and at the same time the brain was the seat of the imagination and insight by means of which he has enjoyed the possibility of entering upon dimensions of life and experience unknown to any other animal.

When prehistorians consider the archaeological evidence for man's emergence as a new kind of animal, they are bound, if they are concerned with its meaning, to ask themselves how it was that in the course of a few tens of thousands of generations a new and specifically human

[93] Whereas the brain capacity of most Australopithecines fell within the upper limit of present-day gorillas, the two main varieties of *Homo erectus* reached *ca.* 950 cc. (Trinil) and 1050 cc. (Pekin), respectively, and Neanderthal Man (*Homo sapiens neanderthalensis*) ranged between *ca.* 1300 and 1650 cc. The fact that the rapid increase in the size of the brain followed and did not precede the assumption of an upright posture was emphasised by H. Vallois in his contribution to S. L. Washburn's *Social Life of Early Man* (London, 1962), pp. 215–217.

[94] In his popular work *Man's Poor Relations* (New York, 1942), Earnest Hooton made the explicit point that: "The rudest savages in the world today far exceed the chimpanzee, mechanically the most gifted ape, in manual skill and dexterity in the manipulation of objects" (p. xxxix). This dexterity he attributed first and foremost to the superior development of man's brain.

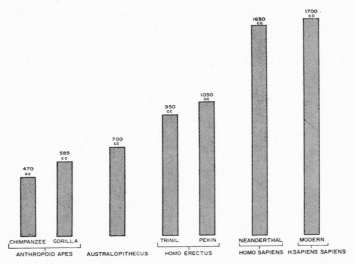

FIG. 5. The growth of the brain in the course of primate evolution

way of life appeared in our universe. Why are we not still a grimacing bunch of nonhuman primates? How and why have the manifold changes that comprised man's prehistory come about? Why have they proceeded at an ever accelerating pace? Why are we still not bashing out pebble tools or even hand axes? How did we come to eat bread? What do the material advances in technology, land occupation, and subsistence portend, and how do we explain them?

Men have, ever since they began to be aware of their context in time, been concerned with how they came to be what they are. Among preliterate peoples the prevailing material culture, social institutions, and even physical environment are commonly accepted as the work of ancestors or culture heroes. As men became literate the origins of all such things came to be ascribed to the creative, innovating achievements of gods and their

59

particular servants, achievements embodied in scriptures or sacred writings. More recently, explanations have returned to the anthropomorphic level, but this time it has no longer been mythological or legendary heroes but unknown artificers or food winners who have been held to have shaped human destiny. Only a generation ago, Gordon Childe entitled a still famous book *Man Makes Himself* and Arnold Toynbee in his *Study of History* constantly returned to the theme of men responding or failing to respond to challenges. It is, indeed, ironical that the image of man entertained by some humanists as the creator of his own destiny has been fed by an exaggerated notion of the role of natural scientists whose achievement has been in reality no more revolutionary than the winning of a partial insight into natural processes. So far as anthropology is concerned, it may be doubted whether an anthropomorphic explanation of prehistory has much to tell us. Indeed, one is compelled to ask whether attempts to dramatise the past in such terms do not interfere with our proper task. Is it really sensible or profitable to think of man as something apart from the world in which he has his being? Are we not really concerned with a process, the process that has not merely shaped men and their cultures, but all other forms of life and indeed our universe and all the other universes of which we are becoming increasingly aware?

It is plain that if we accept the full implications of *The Origin of Species*, if we acknowledge without reserve that man and his works are in truth a product of the same evolutionary forces as have shaped the universe, then we can hardly view him as making himself or challenging nature. The contrary has of course to be faced that, if man really made himself, then it would be a waste of time to consider prehistory in any other light than as an almost hopelessly defective kind of history. To a historian with full documentary and biographical sources it is possible to treat history as a kind of morality play: the characters appear briefly on the stage, interact with others, make their choices, and submit to the judgement of the historian. In such a play particularity of persons and circumstances is everything; but it is precisely this which is by definition beyond the reach of the prehistorian. The wise student of man's past must observe a certain tact if he is not to waste his time; above all he should confine himself to problems capable of being solved by the kind of evidence likely to be available. In studying the prehistoric past it is often futile or at least highly uneconomic to ask the kind of question that most keenly engages social anthropologists or the historians of literate societies. A sound argument for studying prehistory in the context of anthropology is surely that it facilitates a rational allocation of research goals. A main contribution that prehistorians can make to the general understanding is to investigate the operation over much longer periods of time than are available to social anthropologists or even to historians of the processes involved in the evolution of human society.

The thesis I would seek to propound is quite simply that man and his way of life as this has developed down to the present day are both ultimately the product of natural selection. In saying this one has, of course, to make many reservations. It hardly needs emphasizing that, whereas biological evolution has proceeded on a genetic basis, cultural evolution rests on a social basis. Culture is shared and transmitted by virtue of belonging to particular communities that are in themselves constituted by sharing particular traditions. Natural selection could nevertheless operate on cultural variations as well as on genetic mutations. As we shall see (p. 98), cultural diversity was by no means the only source of variability in human society; the emergence and enrichment of human personality was another potent source of deviation on which the forces of natural selection could play. A fact of the utmost significance in so far as social evolution is concerned is that the powers of articulate speech and in the long run of writing and electronics, by facilitating the storing and accumulation of information, have caused cultural evolution in the world at large to accelerate at an ever increasing pace.

It is fortunate that the aspect of human behaviour which has left its clearest imprint on the archaeological record is that concerned with technology and subsistence, since it is precisely in the context of economic life that natural selection has operated most clearly and demonstrably. The records of economic life are as much there for study as are the bones of extinct animals. Prehistorians are indeed cultural paleontologists. The artifacts on which prehistoric archaeologists have to work are veritable fossils of human life. Tools, after all, were used to manipulate and shape the environment; clothes and their fastenings, not to mention houses, to provide shelter; weapons to hunt wild animals and contend with other men in the spacing out of territory; digging sticks, spades, and ploughs for cultivating the ground; and skis, sledges, wheeled vehicles, and boats for traversing land and water. The use of these and the many other categories of material equipment is not in doubt. In Childe's vivid analogy man's implements and indeed his whole material equipment can be regarded as extra-corporeal limbs. They serve his purposes as an organism. The fact that men shaped their flints and stones in accordance with socially inherited traditions, whereas lions and tigers owe their teeth and claws to genetic inheritance, does not alter the fact that the biological effectiveness of artifacts as of physical attributes is determined by their fitness for the task in hand. In relation to human society, natural selection has operated through the economic arrangements by which men have sought to extract a living from the world in which they live.

As a prehistoric archaeologist, it is reassuring to discover that this point of view is shared by physical anthropologists or at least by those who, like those of whom Professor Sherwood L. Washburn is a conspicuous leader, seek the explanation of successful fossil forms in terms of behavioural change and appreciate that the environment to which the *Hominidae* adapted was one increasingly shaped by culture. I count myself particularly fortunate that after completing the text of these lectures I had the opportunity of reading Dr. Bernard Campbell's *Human Evolution*.[95] The measure of confirmation I found there only supports the conclusion that what matters in science is the approach rather than

[95] *Human Evolution: An Introduction to Man's Adaptations* (London and Chicago, 1967).

the field of specialisation. If one approaches by way of
the ecological context of fossils, one might well be
tempted to carry the matter to a logical conclusion and
characterise the genus *Homo* as a product of culture and
thus in a sense as domesticated. If it remains true that
the bare possibility of man depended on a long sequence
of Primate behaviour both in the trees and on the
ground, the rapidity of his evolution during the Pleistocene is most readily explained in terms of the evolution
of his culture, in respect of his subsistence, of his technology, and—at a certain stage—of dramatic extensions
in his zone of settlement.

If it is true that human culture developed by insensible
graduations from the behaviour of earlier genera of
Primates, it could hardly be expected that archaeology
would reveal a clear break between the utilization of
whatever materials lay at hand and the shaping of natural
objects to make them easier to grasp and more effective
to use, any more than there was a clear break between
man and other Primates in the paleontological record,
whether physically or in the use of tools.[96] Sticks must
have been among the earliest tools, and it would only
have been necessary to point straight pieces of wood to
make spears capable of giving man the advantage over
other animals stronger than himself on which his future
depended. Unfortunately wood, like so many of the materials used by man with a simple technology, is highly

[96] K. R. L. Hall, "Tool-Using Performances as Indicators of
Behavioral Adaptability," *Primates: Studies in Adaptation and
Behavioral Variability*, ed. Phyllis C. Jay (New York, 1968), pp.
131–148.

perishable. The fact that so far the earliest spears yet discovered date from the Middle Pleistocene[97] (see Fig. 6)
in no wise lessens the probability that this weapon was
among the earliest known to man. Other materials that
must have come readily to hand, as early man extended
his mastery over other species by hunting, were animal
bones or the splinters from such that would arise from
breaking them open for extracting marrow. There is
evidence that such were used at a very early stage, even,
it has been argued by some, by the australopithecines of
Makapansgat.[98]

On the other hand, any elaborate shaping of organic
material tough enough to be of much use for tools and

[97] The first example to be recognised was recovered from an
interglacial deposit of peaty loam at Clacton, Essex, England, and
comprised the upper 38 cm. of a yew shaft having a carefully
pointed tip; see *Proceedings of the Prehistoric Society of East
Anglia*, vol. 3, pt. 4. A second find, that recovered from between
the ribs of a straight-tusked elephant (*Hesperoloxodon antiquus*
Falc.) in an interglacial deposit at Lehringen, near Verden in
Lower Saxony, Germany, survived to a length of 2.4 m. and had
a tapered point hardened in the fire; see Hallam J. Movius, *Southwestern Journal of Anthropology*, 6 (1950), 139–142.

[98] See Philip V. Tobias, "Cultural Hominization Among the
Earliest African Pleistocene Hominids," *Proceedings of the Pre-
historic Society*, 33 (1967), 367–376. More convincing evidence is
that adduced by the Abbé Breuil from the deposits at Choukoutien; see H. Breuil, "Bone and Antler Industry of the Choukoutien: *Sinanthropus* Site," *Palaeontologia Sinica*, n.s. D, no. 6
(Pekin, 1939). For a wide-ranging discussion, see Raymond A.
Dart, "The Abbé Breuil and the Osteodontokeratic Culture," in
Miscelanea en Homenaje al Abate Henri Breuil, ed. E. Ripoll
Perelló (Barcelona, 1964–1965), 1:347–361. It should be added
that the case argued by Dart is by no means generally accepted
among prehistorians.

0   25   50 cm

FIG. 6. Wooden spears of Middle Pleistocene age: (upper) pointed tip from Clacton, England *(after British Museum)*; (lower) more or less complete spear from Lehringen, Saxony, Germany *(after Movius)*

weapons would have involved the use of hard and readily available substances, such as flint or stone. From a paleontological point of view, such materials have the enormous advantage that they survive under almost any conditions though frequently undergoing surface changes. Of course flint and stone tools pose many problems of interpretation quite apart from that of their precise use. The difficulty of deciding whether man has used particular unmodified lumps of stone is under most circumstances insoluble. Indeed, it is not always even a simple matter to decide whether particular flakes have been struck by man fashioning a tool or accidentally by one of the several agencies, climatic or mechanical, capable of producing similar results.[99] The fact remains that flint and stone

[99] Thus, the flakes exposed on the foreshore at the foot of the cliffs at Cromer, Norfolk, England, which were at one time held to constitute a distinct Paleolithic industry, the "Cromerian," are now generally interpreted as the product of wave action on the beach. Again, pebbles from the Batoka Gorge, Zambia, which closely resemble the so-called Kafuan industry of Uganda, have been explained by Dr. Desmond Clark as having been shaped by

tools, being abundant, relatively imperishable, and amenable to a variety of techniques of working, provide a record of technological change of unexampled duration and value.

It follows from what has been said earlier (p. 62) about the nature of human culture that it can hardly have developed along a course of unilinear evolution. Social evolution was polycentric, developing in many distinct though interconnected areas. The immense range of environments occupied by man would alone ensure that natural selection would result in a variety of cultural manifestations at any one moment of time. But this is not the only reason why we do not see mankind everywhere developing along uniform lines; one has to remember that every advance in the complexity of social life opened up an increasingly large number of alternatives. The existence of distinct cultural manifestations in neighbouring territories—and at an advanced stage of social evolution at different levels in the same communities— was of extreme importance from an evolutionary point of view, because it offered a wide range of alternatives on which the process of selection could play. Although economic competition was never perfect between human societies, it nevertheless existed and in the long term it provided the most important medium through which selection could operate. In practice this competition between alternative answers to analogous problems occurred much more often in the context of peaceful ac-

the purely natural process of "direct percussion brought about by rocks falling from above"; see *Proceedings of the Prehistoric Society,* 24 (1958), 64–77.

culturation than in that of conflict. Indeed, it might be said that up to a point frequency and intensity of culture contact was a controlling factor in cultural development; for no significant human societies have ever existed permanently in complete isolation, and those most cut off from contacts were as a rule those most marginal to centers of rapid advance.

This and the fact that the main drift of evolution in the sphere of economics has been in the same direction, that is toward obtaining the maximum return for the minimum expenditure of effort, means that behind the diversity of cultural expression it should in fact be possible to discern underlying regularities. In the context of world history it is for some purposes the regularities rather than the idiosyncracies that are most directly relevant. In the realm of the lithic industries that provide the skeletal framework of the technology for all but the last two hundred and fifty generations of men, it is useful for some purposes to distinguish a series of modes. The idea that the basic modus operandi of prehistoric industries has undergone a broad development in time is one that has been entertained by distinguished archaeologists in the past in relation to both lithic and metallurgical technology.[100] In relation to flint and stone working, the evidence is now clearer and full enough to justify further consideration.

[100] For example, in his Huxley Memorial Lecture for 1944, "Archaeological Ages as Technological Stages," Gordon Childe distinguished four modes (0,1–3) in the working of copper and bronze and two in that of iron. *Journal of the Royal Anthropological Institute*, 74 (1944), 1–19.

In reviewing the succession of modes that trans-
cended cultural idioms in lithic production, one must
bear in mind certain qualifications. First it is hardly to
be expected that lithic industries should necessarily be
sharply defined from one another. Techniques that,
when applied on a broad front, helped to define a new
mode might be and in fact normally were present or
latent in earlier ones,[101] only coming forward as dominant traits when selected to fill a newly emerged need;
and on the other hand methods dominant in one mode
were frequently combined with those of later ones, re-
sulting in industries that might be classified as hybrids
of two or even more modes. Yet the fact that the lithic
industries made and used by particular communities
rarely conform narrowly to any one mode does not in-
validate the concept for certain kinds of discourse. The
second main qualification to be born in mind is that not
all our modes were of universal occurrence. Indeed, we
know that none were, even if certain techniques were, so
to speak, incorporated in the general heritage of man-

[101] To quote only two examples, there is first the fact that mode
4 was anticipated locally and briefly by the appearance in Cyre-
naica and Palestine of blades or blade-like flakes underlying industries in mode 3. See references to "Pre-Aurignacian" industries
in D. A. E. Garrod, *Cambridge Ancient History*, fasc. 30, 11 f.;
and C. B. M. McBurney, *The Haua Fteah* (Cambridge, 1967), p.
96. As a second instance, the appearance of more or less complete
and highly polished axe- and adze-blades characteristic of mode 6
was to some extent anticipated by the appearance of edge-ground
stone tools in Early Stone Age contexts in Australia and in Early
Jomon deposits in Japan. See D. J. Mulvaney, *The Prehistory of
Australia* (London, 1969), p. 110; J. Edward Kidder, *Japan Before
Buddhism* (London, 1959), p. 54.

kind. We have to remember that in the course of pre-history the habitat of man underwent a great expansion so that the first modes were practiced in their pristine manner only in the cortical zone of the hominids. Conversely, it may well be that modes 3 and 4 emerged as a result of natural selection in the more northerly territories occupied during the Upper Pleistocene.

Mode 1 (see Fig. 7).—The earliest method of working flint or stone tools was extremely elementary. The stone-worker merely hammered off a few flakes from a pebble or other nodule. In this way he might produce flake tools that might be used even without further retouch and heavier forms that could have been used for chopping, cutting, or scraping. Industries in this mode occur in Lower or early Middle Pleistocene deposits over the warmer parts of the Old World from Africa and Europe to Southwest Asia and North China, to which human settlement appears to have been confined at this time.[102]

Mode 2.—A new mode was established during the Middle Pleistocene when flint and stone knappers ex-

[102] The best descriptions of mode 1 industries from Africa are those by M. D. Leakey dealing with materials from beds 1 and 2 at Olduvai and by M. Biberson in relation to the sequence in Morocco; see pp. 417–446 and 447–475 of *Background to Evolution in Africa*, eds. Walter Bishop and J. Desmond Clark (London, 1967). The most convenient reference for Asia is still Hallam L. Movius in *Transactions of the American Philosophical Society*, n.s. 38 (1948); but see also D. Walker and Ann de G. Sieveking, "The Palaeolithic Industry of Kota Tampan, Malaya," *Proceedings of the Prehistoric Society*, 28 (1962), 103–139.

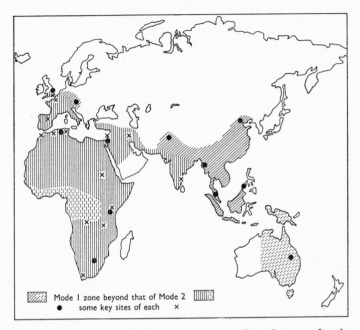

FIG. 7. Map showing approximate extents of modes 1 and 2 in lithic technology. Since mode 1 continued to be practised by the makers of some mode 2 industries, it is difficult to map the extent of mode 1 industries at all precisely except where they were practised beyond the range of mode 2. Some key sites are plotted for each mode.

extended secondary flaking over both faces of the residual tool. Quite plainly this mode stemmed from the preceding one and presumably arose because it provided more effective tools that would for this reason have been selected for survival in the normal course of evolution. Where a succession of industries can be established, as in parts of North Africa and in the Rift Valley of East Africa, it is possible to observe the appearance first of the bifacial flaking technique and then of the extension of this over the whole or the greater part of both faces of the nodule in such a way as to expand the effective perimeter.[103]

Industries characterised above all by bifacial hand axes were concentrated in southern Europe and Africa with parts of Southwest Asia and peninsular India. Within this tradition there is evidence in some areas for progressive refinement in technique during the course of time, and there was obviously scope for wide variation in relation to local ecological circumstances.[104] Bifacial techniques failed to spread as far east as China and Southeast Asia; in these territories industries continued to be made in mode 1 and it was these that were first carried to Australia.[105]

Mode 3 (see Fig. 8).—At a fairly early stage of the Upper Pleistocene, a new mode developed in an area overlapping the northern part of the handaxe zone in North Africa, Europe, and parts of Southwest Asia[106] and ex-

---

[103] For instance, Biberson says in his *Le Paléolithique Inférieur du Maroc Atlantique* (Rabat, 1961), "we know that, by gradual transition, a Handaxe Culture replaced the Pebble Culture at the beginning of the Middle Pleistocene" (p. 466). Cf. M. D. Leakey, *Background to Evolution*, p. 438.

[104] For instance, in the small almond-shaped axes of the Fauresmith industries of the early Upper Pleistocene in South Africa or the long pick-like forms of the Lupemban culture of equatorial Africa dating from the later Upper Pleistocene.

[105] Corresponding to the Early Stone Age of Australia as defined in *World Prehistory: A New Outline* (Cambridge, 1969), pp. 253–254.

[106] Comprising the Mousterian, Levalloisian, and Levalloiso-Mousterian assemblages. See C. B. M. McBurney, *Proceedings of the Prehistoric Society*, 16 (1950), 173–178 and *The Stone Age of*

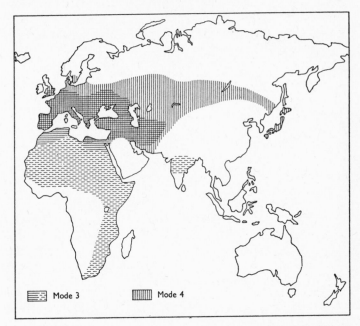

Mode 3   Mode 4

FIG. 8. Map showing approximate extents of modes 3 and 4 of
Old World lithic technology. In the case of mode 3 a distinction is made between the cortical area (Levallois,
Mousterian, and Levalloiso-Mousterian) shown in solid
shading and the peripheral (Aterian, Still Bay, and Fauresmith, the latter having a strong element of mode 2.

tending into the newly settled territories of South Russia[107] as far east as Uzbekistan.[108] The emphasis lay on the

Northern Africa (London, 1960), chap. 4; also D. A. E. Garrod in
Cambridge Ancient History, vol. 1 fasc. 30 (Cambridge, 1965),
pp. 3–22.

[107] For a useful summary for European Russia, see Richard G.
Klein, "The Mousterian of European Russia," *Proceedings of the
Prehistoric Society*, 35 (1969).

[108] Hallam J. Movius, "The Mousterian Cave of Teshik-Tash,
South-eastern Uzbekistan, Central Asia," *American School of
Prehistoric Research Bulletin*, 17 (1953), 11–71.

production of flakes from carefully prepared cores. In some industries these were shaped like a tortoise so that a flake could be struck from the convex face in a form ready for immediate use, though for particular purposes these might be trimmed on one or two edges to make "points" or "scrapers"; in others, cores might be of simpler disc form; and in either case industries might or might not be accompanied by hand axes carried forward from mode 2. In the course of time mode 3 techniques penetrated almost the whole of the former hand axe territory of Africa, in parts of which they, indeed, became dominant.[109] Again, there is evidence for a marked trend toward the use of flake tools struck from prepared cores in peninsular India.[110]

Mode 4.—A significant change occurred with the appearance between 30 and 40 thousand years ago of industries based on the production of regular blades[111] struck by a punch technique from carefully prepared elongated cores. These formed blanks from which a much greater variety of objects could be shaped, including knives, end scrapers, projectile points, and gravers or

[109] See industries of the First Intermediate and Middle Stone Age of Sub-Saharan Africa; J. Desmond Clark, *The Prehistory of Southern Africa* (London, 1959), 142 ff.

[110] Constituting the "Middle Paleolithic" or "Middle Stone Age" industries of Indian prehistorians; see H. D. Sankalia, *Prehistory and Protohistory in India and Pakistan* (Bombay, 1962), chap. 2. Many flakes have prepared platforms and the tortoise core, though rare, is present (p. 100 and fig. 47, 4).

[111] Equivalent to the Advanced or Upper Paleolithic of European prehistorians (*World Prehistory: A New Outline*, chap. 3).

burins.[112] These last may well have been developed mainly for cutting up and shaping animal bone, antler, and ivory, of which much more sophisticated use was made by practitioners of mode 4 industries;[113] and, again, for engraving representations on antler and bone artifacts and on rock surfaces in executing the art recovered from an extensive territory from Iberia to Siberia. The new mode apparently developed within the territory of the preceding one, but it was evidently carried by pioneers over extensive territories to the north and east. In European Russia, settlement extended to 55 degrees north; and east of the Urals, bearers of a mode 4 technology, pressed into Japan,[114] northeastern Siberia[115] and the New World.[116] In many industries of

[112] The varying shapes and proportions of these, as of the accompanying artifacts of antler and bone, from successive layers of the French caves led French prehistorians to designate a number of cultures named after localities where they happen to have been well represented. To begin with, this nomenclature was applied outside western Europe; but as archaeology has matured in other continents local sequences have been defined by terms taken from indigenous localities.

[113] E.g. *Proceedings of the Prehistoric Society*, 19 (1953), 148–160.

[114] See, for example, S. Sugihara, *The Stone Age Remains at Iwajuku, Gumma Pref., Japan* (Tokyo: Meiji University, 1956); M. Tozawa "Preceramic Industry with Knife-Blades of Sunagawa, Saitama Pref.," *Memoirs of the Tokyo Archaeological Society*, vol. 4, no. 1 (Tokyo, 1968), 1–42; C. Serizawa, "The Chronology of Palaeolithic Industries and Carbon 14 Dates in Japan," *Reports of the Research Institute for Japanese Culture, Tohoku University, Sendai, Japan*, no. 3, 1967.

[115] The site of Mal'ta, *ca.* 80 m. NW of Irkutsk—well known for its figurines, ornaments and implements made from ivory and bone, as well as for its dwellings—yielded blade tools, including

this mode use continued to be made of the bifacial technique of mode 2 for such special purposes as projectile points; and in some, these points were the most immediately prominent features.[117] Other mode 4 industries, for instance in Siberia, were enriched by techniques proper to mode 3.[118]

Mode 5.—Certain industries of mode 4 included an element of small, often minute, flints (microliths) shaped by the same blunting technique as some larger forms. At the close of the Ice Age and during the Neothermal period this element, and the various forms of slotted haft for which they were designed, became so prominent that one may justly speak of a distinctive mode. Industries in

---

burins, points, and end-scrapers; see *Paleolit SSSR*, ed. P. Efimenko (Moscow, 1935), fig. 22, 5. On the other hand the Lena Valley sites published by A. P. Okladnikov in *The Archaeology and Geomorphology of Northern Asia*, ed. Henry N. Michael (Toronto, 1964), pp. 33–39, have so far produced only a rather nondescript lithic industry.

[116] American prehistorians have, in the past, concentrated mainly on projectile points when studying the Paleoindian phase, but the blades from Clovis published by F. E. Green (*American Antiquity*, 29 [1951], 255–268) and the burins from many localities are diagnostic of mode 4.

[117] E.g. the Solutrean of Europe or the Paleoindian variants in North America.

[118] Thus the industry from Afontova Gora II, near Krasnoyarsk, included tortoise cores and points and scrapers of Mouterian character alongside burins, "button" scrapers, and bladelets with steep retouch—thus, mode 3/4. See N. K. Auerbach et al., *Travaux de la Commission du Quaternaire de l'académie des sciences de l'URSS*, 1 (Leningrad, 1932), 45–113.

mode 5 are of particular interest because they were dominant in the Old World during the period of transition
from economies based on hunting and gathering to those
depending at least to some degree on farming. The de-
vice of composite weapons with inset microliths was
widely adopted over Southwest Asia,[119] Europe,[120] extensive tracts of Africa,[121] and southern and eastern
Asia,[122] whence they spread on the one hand to Australia[123] and on the other to the Arctic territories of Alaska,
northern Canada, and Greenland.[124]

Mode 6.—The last significant and widespread mode of
working flint and stone was marked by highly polished
axes or adzes, which first became of crucial importance

[119] *World Prehistory: A New Outline*, chap. 4.

[120] Also Garrod and Clark, *Cambridge Ancient History*, vol. 1,
fasc. 30 (Cambridge, 1965).

[121] J. Desmond Clark, *The Prehistory of Southern Africa* (London, 1959), chap. 7.

[122] See H. D. Sankalia, *Prehistory and Protohistory in India and
Pakistan* (Bombay, 1962), chap. 3; also Bridget Allchin, *The Stone-
Tipped Arrow* (London, 1966). But it cannot be accepted that
lunates necessarily imply the use of the bow, as their occurrence in
the Middle Stone Age of Australia, a continent in which the use
of the bow was apparently unknown, well shows.

[123] Microliths were an outstanding feature of the Australian
Middle Stone Age. See *World Prehistory: A New Outline*, pp. 255–
256.

[124] A useful reference is J. L. Giddings, *The Archaeology of Cape
Denbigh* (Providence, 1964), chaps. 4–5 and map 60. For an earlier
occurrence at Onion Portage on the Kobuk river, NW Alaska, see
the same author's posthumous *Ancient Men of the Arctic* (London,
1967), chap. 16.

in habitats supporting a climax vegetation of forest trees. Experiments have shown that polished flint axes were able to fell trees with less effort than ones with chipped edges.[125] Thus, under circumstances in which tree-felling was important, polished blades would be favoured by natural selection over merely chipped ones. This applied with special force where farming was carried on in a forested landscape, since woodland had to be cleared for cultivation and the creation of pasture.[126] It is hardly surprising to find polished stone blades playing an important role in the peasant societies of southwest and southern Asia,[127] as well as in the Far East;[128] in Mediterranean and temperate Europe;[129] over much of Africa;[130] in Mesoamerica and parts of temperate North

[125] See "Farmers and Forests in Neolithic Europe," *Antiquity*, 19 (1945), 68.

[126] See "Forest Clearance and Prehistoric Farming," *Economic History Review*, 17 (1947), 45–51.

[127] See e.g., J. Mellaart, *Çatal Hüyük: A Neolithic Town in Anatolia* (London, 1967), p. 214; E. Anati, *Palestine Before the Arabs* (London, 1963), pp. 267, 271; V. G. Childe, *New Light on the Most Ancient East*, 4th ed. (London, 1952), figs. 56, 59; R. E. M. Wheeler, *Ancient India*, 4 (1948), 180–310; and B. K. Thapar, "Neolithic Problem in India," in *Indian Prehistory: 1964*, eds. V. N. Misra and M. S. Mate (Poona, 1965), pp. 87–112.

[128] See Cheng Te-K'un, *Prehistoric China* (Cambridge, 1959), figs. 18, 20, and pls. 9–13; J. E. Kidder, *Japan Before Buddhism* (London, 1959), p. 99 and fig. 23.

[129] V. G. Childe, *The Dawn of European Civilization*, 6th ed. (London, 1957), *passim*.

[130] G. Caton-Thompson, *The Desert Fayum* (London, 1935), pls. 9 and 22; A. K. Arkell, *Shaheinab* (Oxford, 1953), pls. 18–19; T. Shaw, *Proceedings of the Prehistoric Society*, 10 (1944), 28–62; J. D. Clark, *The Prehistory of Southern Africa*, pp. 191–192.

America;[131] in New Guinea and Melanesia;[132] and not least in Polynesia,[133] where they were additionally important for shaping the canoes without which the islands could hardly have been occupied. But the use of polished stone blades was by no means confined to societies based on farming; it was, for instance, a basic component of the culture of the hunter-fishers of the circumpolar zone of the northern hemisphere.[134]

Another closely associated sphere in which progress has been made lies in the taking into use of more effective raw materials. Even at the remote period represented by the early living areas at Olduvai there is evidence for considerable discrimination in the choice of materials for stone implements, something which, after all, is hardly surprising when one takes account of the

[131] For eastern North America, see Gordon R. Willey, *An Introduction to American Archaeology* (New Jersey, 1966), 1:272, 276; fig. 5–46. A striking instance from Mesoamerica is the cache of finely polished stone axes from the Pre-Classic site of La Venta, see P. Drucker et al., "Excavations at La Venta, Tabasco," *Bureau of American Ethnology Bulletin*, 170 (Washington, 1959); for Panama, see *Handbook of South American Indians*, vol. 4, pl. 20.c. Not surprisingly, polished stone axes are associated with the slash and burn agriculture of Amazonia; see C. Evans in *Prehistoric Man in the New World*, eds. Jennings and Norbeck (Chicago, 1964), p. 427.

[132] See the present author's "Traffic in Stone Axe and Adze Blades," *Economic History Review*, 18 (1965), 18–21; also *Proceedings of the Prehistoric Society*, 32 (1966), 96–121.

[133] Cf. Roger Duff's "Neolithic Adzes of Eastern Polynesia" in *Anthropology in the Southern Seas*, eds. J. D. Freeman and W. R. Geddes (New Plymouth, N.Z., 1959), pp. 121–148.

[134] See G. Gjessing, *Circumpolar Stone Age* (Copenhagen, 1944).

adaptive value of more effective implements and tools. As we are reminded by recent studies on the distribution of obsidian in Southwest Asia, there is evidence that already during the Late Pleistocene raw materials of special merit were being obtained from a distance; the hunters of the Zagros zone, for example, were already drawing obsidian (see Fig 9) from sources near Lake Van in eastern Turkey.[135] Again the vital role of stone axe and adze blades during the prevalence of mode 6 is reflected in the way raw materials of special merit were mined or quarried and distributed over great distances, something best documented from Neolithic Europe[136] but also well exemplified from New Guinea,[137] New South Wales,[138] and New Zealand.[139]

A most significant advance came when men first learned how to extract metals from ores and work them into more effective weapons and tools, something which was hardly possible until settled life had been sufficiently well established to make it possible to support a specialised craft of smiths and which likewise implied a more or less extensive network of exchange. Although copper

[135] J. R. Cann and C. Renfrew, *Proceedings of the Prehistoric Society*, 30 (1964), 111–133; C. Renfrew et al., *ibid.*, 32 (1966), 30–72 and 34 (1968), 319–331.

[136] *Prehistoric Europe: The Economic Basis* (London, 1952), pp. 245 ff.

[137] J. Chappell, "Stone Axe Factories in the Highlands of East New Guinea," *Proceedings of the Prehistoric Society*, 32 (1966), 96–121.

[138] Work pioneered in the Tamworth-Grafton area of New South Wales by Dr. Isabel McBryde of the University of New England.

[139] *Economic History Review*, 18 (1965), 1 ff.

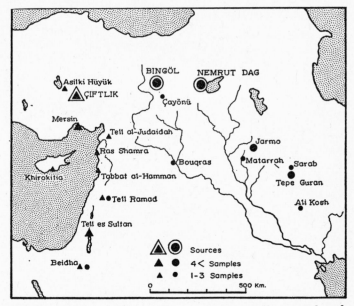

FIG. 9. Traffic in obsidian from certain sources in central and eastern Anatolia to the Zagros and the Levant in the 7th and 6th millennia B.C. *(adapted from Renfrew and Cann)*

and its alloys helped to shape the technology of all the ancient Old World civilizations of Mesopotamia, Egypt, Greece, India, and China, the use of copper or bronze for implements was quite unknown in the prehistory of large parts of Africa, the whole of Australia, and the Pacific; and if we exclude the use of native copper by the Old Copper culture of Minnesota, Wisconsin, and Michigan,[140] the only metallurgical industry established in the New World by the time of the conquest was that developed in the Andean zone. It is especially worthy of note with regard to the stress laid on the polycentric na-

[140] S. W. Miles, "A Revaluation of the Old Copper Industry," *American Antiquity*, 16 (1951), 240–247.

ture of social evolution, that the Maya—for all the monumentality of their architecture, their calendrical virtuosity, and their script—still relied on stone as the basis of their technology. In much of the Old World, on the other hand, metallurgy played a more vital role. Thus bronze and copper metallurgy was in early times restricted to the territories that were soon to give birth to higher civilizations or to lands which came under the influence of these; and the working of iron, though it began within the zone of bronze metallurgy, spread over extensive territories in Africa, Southern India, and Indonesia—areas that had previously relied on stone. Another illustration of polycentricity is the fact that, whereas in the West early iron metallurgy was based on forging, and casting only came in with the approach of the modern industrial age, in Chou China iron working was from the first based on the casting technique.[141]

The advances in technology incorporating new methods of production and the utilization of a wider range of raw materials made it possible for *Homo sapiens* to expand his range of settlement and occupy a wider range of environments. As we have noted, *Homo erectus*, who depended on industries in modes 1 and 2, was mainly confined to the relatively warm territories long occupied by nonhuman primates, even though he had already, early in the Middle Pleistocene, occupied lands sufficiently far north to place a selective advantage on the use and production of fire. Some further northward expansion was achieved by *Homo sapiens neanderthalen-*

[141] William Watson, *China Before the Han Dynasty* (London, 1961), p. 144.

sis, who disposed of mode 3 industries that included specialised scraping equipment of a kind well adapted to the preparation of animal skins for clothing and shelter. A dramatic expansion, involving broad tracts of northern Eurasia and extending into the New World, was left to modern man *(Homo sapiens sapiens)* who in his northern territories disposed in the closing stages of the Upper Pleistocene of the more advanced industries made possible by the adoption of mode 4 techniques. Finally, it was the adoption of mode 6, making it comparatively easy to shape the timbers of sea-going boats, that made it possible for man to traverse even extensive tracts of the Pacific Ocean and occupy islands over its surface.

Broad changes can likewise be seen in the realm of subsistence. The first change and one that in a sense symbolized the appearance of man was the shift from an almost exclusively vegetarian diet to one in which animal protein came to play a role of substantial importance. Like all attempts at historical reconstruction and like much of the rest of human knowledge, this change is still hypothetical; the existing great apes are certainly not the first ancestors of man, and the diet of these ancestors is still unknown. Nevertheless, it is at least suggestive that the great apes, though basically dependent on plant food, relish animal protein when it comes their way,[142] which suggests that they were vegetarian more by

[142] This point has been well made by Adolph H. Schultz in *Social Life of Early Man,* ed. S. L. Sherwood (London, 1962), p. 83; "Most prosimians and some New World monkeys eat more worms, insects, frogs, lizards and birds' eggs than plants."

circumstance than by choice. Thanks to the researches of Dr. and Mrs. Leakey at Olduvai, it appears that already during the Lower Pleistocene certain forms of Australopithacine (*A. africanus* cf *Homo habilis*) were supplementing their predominantly vegetarian diet by small animals like lizards, rodents, and birds, as well as by scavenging big game. It was the shaping of effective weapons, notably wooden spears, that first made it possible for certain primates to hunt animals, in some cases more powerful than themselves, and the ability to do so effectively marked them as men. In terms of economic activity the change of diet implied a shift from a monotonous routine of foraging to one in which this basic activity was complemented by hunting. Socially this was of the utmost significance because, whereas the routine of foraging was shared equally by both sexes and by individuals of all ages, the addition of hunting led to increased differentiation in the roles of male and female in the food quest: hunting was an activity to which man, the more active partner in sexual relationships and physically more powerful because selected for this role of dominance, was by his very nature better adapted. The hunting of big game did far more than underline and deepen the economic partnership of the sexes, a basis of the institution of the human family; by necessitating the cooperation of several males it promoted the development of social groupings comprising a number of family units.

The key importance of hunting became even more manifest after early man had penetrated territories lying to the north of what might be termed the homeland

of the primates. A crucial pioneering role was played by
the peoples who first occupied the northern marches of
the Paleolithic world and whose principal memorials are
lithic industries in mode 3,[143] but it was not until between 30 and 40 thousand years ago that we find clear
evidence among the makers of mode 4 industries of a
pronounced intensification in the activity of hunting.
This took the form both of a more highly differentiated
weaponry (see Fig. 10) and of a graphic art which, whatever else is said about it, bears witness to an intense observation of and identification with wild animals. Some
of the most splendid memorials of the advanced hunters
of the Late Glacial period in parts of western Europe
were the representations of game animals on the walls
and ceilings of caves like Altamira and Lascaux.

A further change and one that underlay and made
possible the development of the various literate civilizations of man was the adoption of farming. The crucial
significance of what Gordon Childe[144] once termed the
"Neolithic Revolution" is amply documented in the
archaeological record. No society dependent on catching
or gathering has ever achieved literate civilization on its
own; and, conversely, all literate civilizations can be
seen to have developed from and still to depend ultimately upon the practice of farming. This fact is undis-
puted, and Childe more than any other scholar established it as part of conventional wisdom. If today we
regard the change as less a revolution than a gradual

[143] See notes 107 and 108, p. 73.
[144] E.g., *What Happened in History*, 2nd ed. (London, 1954),
pp. 48 ff.

85

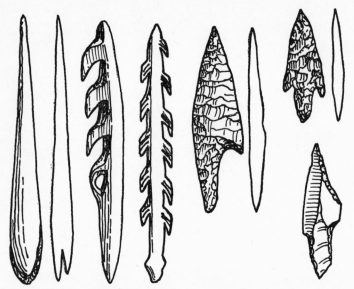

FIG. 10. Weapon heads (spears, harpoons, and arrows) from mode
4 assemblages in Europe

transformation, it should be recognised that this interpretation stems in large measure from field researches by
persons such as Robert Braidwood[145] and R. S. Mac-
Neish[146] in both the Old and New Worlds, for which
Childe's thesis provided the most important single stimulus.

[145] Robert J. Braidwood and Bruce Howe, "Southwestern Asia
Beyond the Lands of the Mediterranean Littoral," in *Courses
Towards Urban Life*, eds. S. Braidwood and Willey (Edinburgh,
1962), pp. 132–146; Braidwood, "The Earliest Village Communities of Southwestern Asia Reconsidered," *Atti VI Congress Inter-
nationale di Scienze Preistoriche e Protostoriche* (Rome, 1962),
2:115–126.

[146] Notably in his researches in the arid Tehuacan Valley of east
central Mexico; see *The Prehistory of the Tehuacan Valley*, vol. 1.
Environment and Subsistence, ed. Douglas S. Byers (Andover,
1967).

Historically speaking, Childe's thesis stemmed from
the contrast drawn by Sir John Lubbock in his *Prehistoric Times* (1865) between Paleolithic hunter-gatherers
and Neolithic farmers, groups held at that time to have
been sundered by a temporal hiatus in Europe, the only
part of the world whose prehistory had then been even
partly explored. The continuity of prehistory has only
been restored by more intensive work in Europe and
above all by the extension of systematic exploration to
the Near East. Nor has this been done merely in a temporal sense. The dichotomy between hunting and gathering on the one hand and stock-raising and agriculture
on the other is no longer so clearly defined as it was by
Lubbock or Childe. The notion that food gatherers were
only capable of grubbing or snatching whatever wild
plant food was going was a stereotype of the way in which
civilized men once regarded those he thought of as primitive. The situation reported by modern field anthropologists is very different. We know that in reality plant
gatherers, like many hunters, required a detailed knowledge of the habits and characteristics of a much greater
variety of species than modern farmers. An inhabitant of
Cape York Peninsula or of the arid interior of Australia
gathers not one or two harvests, but a plentitude in accordance with a pattern far more intricate than that of
our farmers' year.[147] One difference between fully committed farmers and gatherers, in fact, is precisely that
the former in the long-run restrict themselves to a much

---

[147] Donald F. Thomson, "The Seasonal Factor in Human Culture," *Proceedings of the Prehistoric Society,* 5 (1939), 209–221.
See especially pl. 22 and legend.

narrower range of plants, those they have sown themselves. But this change was not a sudden or clear-cut one.

The evidence from prehistory shows that both in the Old and New Worlds, the first sown plants were of relatively minor importance compared with those gathered in the wild. The importance of plants gathered in the wild state did not decline, even for food, until a comparatively late stage in the development of agriculture; indeed in some instances the number of wild plants gathered by early farmers seems even to have increased. Thus, from the Neolithic site of Sipplingen by the Federsee in South Germany, Karl Bertsch identified no fewer than 193 species of plants.[148] These included, in addition to species still cultivated in Europe, seventeen others that have only dropped out of cultivation in recent generations and a much larger number that must have been gathered from forest, lakeside, meadow, and cultivated ground. The practice of farming itself increased the number of plants available for gathering through the creation of meadows and cultivated fields and at the same time created a need for them:[149] for one thing the uncertainty of cereal crops under primitive conditions meant that wild foods were a vital reserve; and for another the developments of technology that accompanied farming led to an increased demand for such things as plant fibres, dyes, and caulking moss. Even at the close of the prehistoric period in Europe during the Roman Iron Age, we find from Hans Helbaek's

[148] See *Badische Fundbericht*, vol. 2 (1932), hft. 9.
[149] *Prehistoric Europe: The Economic Basis* (London, 1952), p. 58.

analysis of the stomach contents of a corpse from Tollund bog and of traces from a more or less contemporary farmstead at Østerbolle, also in Jutland, that the population was consuming a wide range of wild plants as well as cultivated ones.[150]

It was not until the forces of selection operating through subsistence economics made it more profitable to concentrate on sown plants that wild ones ceased to be important for food; and even when this had happened they continued, as we know from the recent peasant cultures of Europe, to be gathered for a great variety of purposes, aromatic, industrial, magical, and medicinal.[151] The determining factor was presumably the adoption of a fully sedentary habit which placed a premium on plants sown close at hand as against those gathered from an extensive range of countryside.

Here again no clear-cut line can be drawn. The discovery by Soviet prehistorians of elaborate house structures on the banks of the great rivers of southern Russia,[152] dating well back into the Upper Pleistocene, the

[150] See Hans Helbaek, "Botanical Study of the Stomach Contents of the Tollund Man," *Aarbøger* (1950), pp. 329–341.

[151] E.g., J. Hoops, *Waldbaume und Kulturpflanzen im germanischen Altertum* (Strasbourg, 1905); H. Brockman–Jerosch, "Die ältesten Nutz- und Kulturpflanzen," *Vierteljahrsschrift der Naturforschung Gesellschaft in Zürich*, Jg. 62 (1917), 80–102; A. Maurizio, *Die Geschichte unserer pflanzennahrung von den Urzeiten bis zur Gegenwart* (Berlin, 1927).

[152] Since the first Upper Paleolithic dwelling sites were found at Gagarino in 1928 by S. N. Zamiatnin, many others have been recognised in southern Russia. See, Eugene A. Golomshtok, *The Old Stone Age in European Russia* (Philadelphia, 1938), pp. 322, 325, 373, 381, 398–401, 435, and 451. More recently, analogous indica-

earliest of them associated with mode 3 industries (see Fig. 11), reminds us that the home base was no invention of farmers. It is of the very essence of humanity to maintain a base where the young can be brought up in the life of culture and to which in consequence food had to be brought for sharing out and consumption. The difference between the home bases of hunter-gatherers and farmers was one of emphasis not of kind. Whereas hunter-gatherers had frequently, like the people of Cape York, to move their families over an extensive territory in the course of the year, the farmer, to the extent that he was committed to the cultivation of one or two crops, was under pressure to settle down in one place. But this development was not sudden or to begin with necessary, as we know from the practices of people who combine the sowing of crops with a migratory habit; just as conversely we hardly need to be reminded of peoples of sedentary habit who yet, like the Indians of the American northwest coast, subsisted on a basis of gathering and hunting.[153]

---

tions have been observed in Mousterian (mode 3) levels at Molodova in the Dnestr Valley; see Richard Klein, *Proceedings of the Prehistoric Society*, 35 (1969). Analogous finds have been made in Siberia at Mal'ta some 85 km. north of Irkutsk (M. M. Gerasimov, "The Palaeolithic Site Mal'ta," in *The Archaeology and Geomorphology of Northern Asia*, ed. Henry N. Michael [Toronto, 1965], pp. 1–32); and at Buret' on the Angara River (A. P. Okladnikov, *Kratkiye soobshcheniya Inst. arkheologii*, 10 [1941], 16–31). Again, dwelling plans have been recovered from Czechoslovakia; see B. Klima, *Dolni Věstonice* (Prague, 1963), pp. 205–210 and figs. 68–69.

[153] C. Daryll Forde, *Habitat, Economy, and Society* 5th ed. (London, 1946), pp. 72 ff.

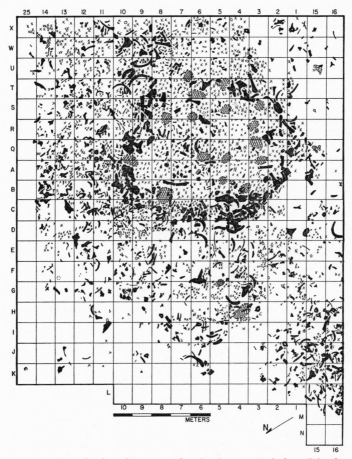

FIG. 11. Plan of refuse from a mode-3 horizon at Molodova I in the valley of the Dnestr, South Russia *(after Klein, redrawn from Chernysh)*

Again, if we turn to the question of sowing as opposed to gathering, we find no clear-cut difference. There is no suggestion that planting the first crop was the result of a bright idea by some deserving pioneer of the human race. Indeed, the distinction between self-propagating and intentionally sown is not merely difficult, but indeed

91

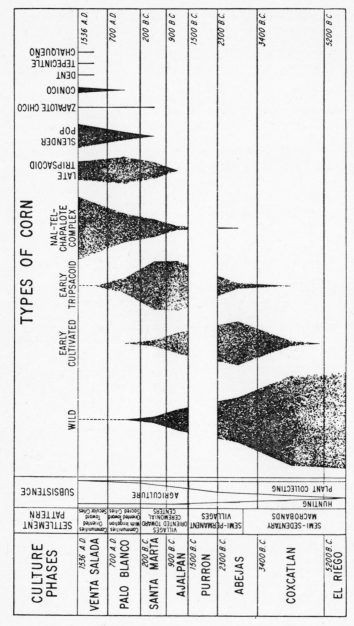

FIG. 12. The evolution of maize in the Valley of Mexico (after Mangelsdorf and MacNeish)

impossible for us to distinguish at this distance in time; it may be doubted whether it was known to prehistoric man himself. The change is surely one to be explained more convincingly in terms of the evolutionary process. If wild plants were brought home, as they must have been to be consumed, they would surely have sown themselves. It is not difficult to imagine that the surroundings of the homestead enriched by domestic refuse, not to mention the dung of livestock, would have provided conditions far more favourable for growth than those occurring in their natural habitats. And this factor would naturally have assumed added importance as settlement became more permanent; for the richer the accumulation of phosphates and nitrogen, the more rewarding the returns of sown crops, which would for this very reason enjoy an adaptive advantage over wild ones. With this in mind it is of interest to consider the analysis of maize cobs recovered from successive carbon-dated horizons in the Valley of Tehuacan, Mexico, carried out by Manglesdorf, MacNeish and others.[154] It is hardly surprising to find that, whereas in the earliest assemblages the cultivated variety was quantitatively of minor importance by comparison with the many wild varieties, in the upper ones it steadily gained upon them and ultimately eliminated them completely (see Fig. 12).

In the case of the cereals on which the earliest agriculture in the Old World depended, we know from the excavations at Mureybit in eastern Syria[155] that wild varie-

[154] P. C. Mangelsdorf, R. S. MacNeish and G. R. Willey, "Domestication of Corn," *Science*, 143 (1964), 538–545.
[155] W. van Zeist and W. A. Casparie, "Wild Einkorn Wheat from

ties were harvested. Experiments by Dr. J. R. Harlan
have shown under good conditions a family could harvest in a few weeks all the wild einkorn it needed for a
year.[156] When the harvest was brought to the home base,
some of it must inevitably have given rise to self-sown
crops, which since they would have grown rankly and
did not have to be carried would have enjoyed an adaptive advantage over ones that had to be harvested in
their natural stands. Most wild grains are attached to
the head by a brittle rachis which ensured a ready dis-
persal of the seed. The easiest method of harvesting these
would have been to tap them into baskets, as the Cali-
fornian Indians used to do with wild seeds.[157] In domesticated cereals, on the other hand, the grains are held in
place by a tough rachis which allows them to be reaped
without too great a loss. We know that in the Near East
cereal crops were harvested from very remote times by
reaping knives[158] having sharp edges formed by one or
more flint blades fixed in a slotted handle of antler, bone,
or wood and held in position by resin. (see Fig. 13). As a

Tell Mureybit in Northern Syria," *Acta botanica Neerlandica*,
17 (1968), 44–53.

[156] "A Wild Wheat Harvest in Turkey," *Archaeology*, 20 (1967),
197–201.

[157] Illustrated by A. L. Kroeber, *Bulletin of the American
Bureau of Ethnology*, no. 78, p. 814 and pl. 24.

[158] E. C. Curwen, *Antiquity*, 15 (1941), 320–336; G. Caton-
Thompson, *The Desert Fayum* (London, 1935), pl. 28, 1, 2 and
20, 1; F. Turville-Petre, *Journal of the Royal Anthropological
Institute*, 62 (1932), 271 ff.; D. A. E. Garrod and D. M. A. Bate,
The Stone Age of Mount Carmel (Oxford, 1937), 1:37, pl. XIII, 1,
3; R. Ghirshman, *Fouilles de Sialk* (Paris, 1938–1939), pl. LV;
R. S. Solecki, *Science*, vol. 139, no. 1551, p. 192, fig. 17; V. M.

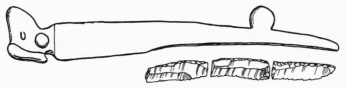

FIG. 13. Bone reaping-knife with flint insets from the Levant (Natufian)

rule the flints were inset end to end and were sometimes squared at the ends to fit, but they might also be set obliquely overlapping one another. How reaping first began, whether it was developed to cope with mutant cereals having a tough rachis, we can only guess. What seems certain is that, once begun, harvesting by reaping would have selected tough rachis cereals for survival.

One could continue in this vein, but enough has been said to make the point that the technology and subsistence of early man was shaped by natural selection operating on cultures adapted to all the various environments in which he lived. Again, it is worth reemphasising that this process could only operate effectively when confronted by variables. It is emphatically not the case that men everywhere and under all circumstances utilized their environment to the limit of their technology. So long as we realise that *Homo economicus* is a lay figure who never, in fact, walked the earth, there is no

Masson, *Antiquity*, 35 (1961), 205, fig. 2; V. von Gonzenbach, *Die Cortaillodkultur in der Schweiz* (Basel, 1949), pl. 10, 3 and 7. Jaw-shaped sickles with handles more or less at right-angles to the cutting-edge came in later with the use of metal, though at first still made of wood with flint insets. See J. G. D. Clark, *Prehistoric Europe* (London, 1952), figs. 52–55.

harm in using him as a model, if only to point up the noneconomic motivations of human behaviour. In reality societies, in so far as they are human, harbour values that are inherited from the past, often from a remote past when quite different forms of economic and social life prevailed. Human beings are prepared to pay a price in terms of economic efficiency to maintain sacred cows of one kind or another. Yet even irrational behaviour, provided it motivates people sufficiently strongly, may in fact have an adaptive value by increasing productivity. Again, ideological, traditional, and other noneconomic patterns of behaviour may be important in another way, simply by increasing the range of variability on which natural selection could play.

In the long run—and prehistorians have to think in terms of long periods of time if they are to make their special contribution to anthropological discourse—it is still true that natural selection operates in favour of those most capable of understanding and exploiting their environment. It is suggestive in this connection that W. W. Rostrow in his key paper[159] on "The Take-off into Self-Contained Growth" has characterised economic growth as being in "the essentially biological field." One is entitled to think that he had it in mind to do more than merely point out the analogy between economic and biological growth; he meant, surely, that economic growth was of the same essential character as biological growth, in the sense that both enlarged the possibilities of life and were subject to the same fundamental process of natural selection and evolution. Basi-

[159] *Economic Journal*, 66 (1956), 25–48.

cally the cultures of which prehistoric archaeologists study the material traces served in their time as mechanisms by means of which communities of men sustained not merely life, but the good life, the life that enshrined values and called forth the greatest effort to realise them. The fact that the production of artifacts was subject to the evolutionary process has obvious implications for the methodology of archaeology. In particular it highlights the need to focus attention on progressive changes in basic processes such as working flint, potting, or metallurgy. From this point of view it is fortunate that modern technology has itself necessitated the development of the conceptual tools and hardware needed for rapid statistical analysis.[160] Imperfect though competition between communities may have been, it seems evident that those people flourished most, and therefore left the main impression on the archaeological record, that were most efficient not merely at a technical level but in terms of social achievement. Natural selection must always and necessarily have favoured those who showed themselves most adaptable to circumstances as these arose and most capable of exerting themselves effectively.

I have spoken of communities and of the processes which shaped the course of their history over long periods of time. What of the individuals who compose societies? Do not human societies differ from animal societies in that they consist of beings capable of thought

[160] For a comprehensive survey of the archaeological implications of these, the reader is referred to Dr. D. L. Clarke's *Analytical Archaeology* (London, 1969).

and of exercising choice? Is one guilty of crass determinism in suggesting that men are subject to the same processes of change that have called into shape not merely the world in which we live, but all those universes that human ingenuity is now allowing us to apprehend?

At this time of day there is surely no need to debate the problem of free will; the statistical models we devise to gain a more precise understanding of the physical world, let alone of social behaviour, take due account of the factors of randomness and deviance. An individual man or for that matter an individual mosquito enjoys at any particular moment a freedom of choice limited only by organic attributes and the constraints of the environment. In relation to evolution, on the other hand, the behaviour of individuals is only relevant in so far as it affects the species or the community.

By and large and under most circumstances, the deviations of individuals have been ineffective in the sense that they have normally failed to deflect or modify social behavior. Yet it is certain that personal dissent has been critically important for the evolution of culture; it provided precisely the variant on which natural selection could operate at some critical juncture in social history, very much as mutations served in the field of biological evolution. When one technique replaced another or when forms were modified, it was not due to some individual innovator so much as to the evolutionary process selecting the individual deviation that happened at some particular juncture to meet the needs of the situation most adequately. In this way, individual departures from the norm might be selected for survival and incorporated into the ongoing and changing pattern of group behaviour.

It is a striking fact that taking the world as a whole, or more accurately the leading centers of innovation, the rate of cultural advance has undergone a marked and progressive acceleration in the course of time. For the earlier ages of mankind, change was so slow that its course could be measured in geological time and could only be detected in the short term by painstaking metrical and statistical analysis. At the same time the earliest industries of man (modes 1 and 2) were remarkable for their homogeneity over vast tracts of territory. It was not until an advanced stage of the Pleistocene that we find evidence for marked local variation and for more rapid change. It is surely no accident that this acceleration and this diversification should have occurred at precisely the same time as convincing evidence arises for self-awareness and by implication for a marked growth in individual thought and feeling. The forces of natural selection had progressively more variables on which to play as cultural traditions grew more complex and diverse and as individuals grew in self-awareness and capacity for thought. The attainment of a settled way of life, based on farming, was another factor to accelerate the pace of change. For one thing the mere fact of being tied to particular localities in itself made for greater regional differences in cultural style. Secondly, as Gordon Childe emphasised, the opportunity that farming gave for people to live and work together in larger communities made it possible for craftsmen to engage in a much greater degree of specialisation, which in itself led

to a larger number of ways of solving particular problems or in other words to a greater range of choice and,
therefore, of variability. Although the civilizations that
developed from the formative stage of settled life shared
certain basic features as a class, it is characteristic of
them that wherever they developed they display idiosyncracies of style and sometimes of form. This is no-
where more clearly displayed than in the scripts (see
Fig. 14) in which their earliest written records were
inscribed. The development of writing—like that of
metallurgy, agriculture, lithic technology, and indeed
almost any manifestation of culture one can think of—
developed along idosyncratic lines in many different
centres. This was eloquently expressed by Henri Frankfort in his comparison of the two earliest literate civilizations of the Old World: "A comparison between
Egypt and Mesopotamia discloses, not only that writing,
representational art, monumental architecture, and a
new kind of political coherence was introduced in the
two countries; it also reveals that the purpose of their
writing, the contents of their representations, the functions of their monumental buildings, and the structure
of their new societies differed completely. What we observe is not merely the establishment of civilized life, but
the emergence, concretely, of the distinctive 'forms' of
Egyptian and Mesopotamian civilization."[161] If the
range of comparison is widened to comprehend, for example, the Indian, Chinese, Greek, and Mayan civilizations, all these points and many others can be made with
even greater force.

[161] *The Birth of Civilization in the Near East* (London, 1951),
p. 49.

FIG. 14. Symbols for ox, earth, and heaven in the pictographic and historic scripts of a. Assyria and b. China

Enough has probably been said to make the point that in the development of modes of subsistence, as of technology, there is no need to envisage culture heroes or revolutions; nor, *pace* Gordon Childe,[162] is it appropriate to think in terms of drama. Instead we are confronted by the same processes as have fashioned ourselves and the universe as a whole; it is merely that they have operated in a different manner. If natural selection functioned in the case of animals through the gene pool, among men it has worked through the medium of culture, most obviously through technology and subsistence patterns, but also through social organisation and value systems. The emergence during modern times of societies in which increasing resources are directed to the

[162] Childe used a consciously theatrical simile on the first page of the second edition of his *New Light on the Most Ancient East* (1952): "There in the Ancient East some episodes at least in the great drama of the conquest of civilization are enacted on the open stage. The greatest moments—that revolution whereby man ceased to be purely parasitic and, with the adoption of agriculture and stock-raising, became a creator emancipated from the whims of his environment, and then, the discovery of metal and the realisation of its properties—have indeed been passed before the curtain rises."

systematic investigation of natural processes has not altered the situation in any fundamental way; it is merely that the process of change has speeded up because the process of natural selection, which operates today to an important degree through state power, has more alternatives from which to choose. Cultural evolution proceeds apace. How or why it started and where it is heading are questions as difficult to answer as how or why it is that our universe began and where it is going. At least we can frame such questions even if we have to admit that we do not know the answers; and framing questions betrays a degree of self-awareness shared by no other animal.

3

The Dawn
of Self-Awareness

Whether any higher animals other than man are self-
conscious is a matter for speculation; but it is safe to
say that man alone has an idea of himself, which plays
an important part in his behaviour.

LORD BRAIN

(From "Science and Behaviour," in *The Advancement of Science*, 1964.)

To those of us who approach prehistory from a broadly anthropological rather than from an art-historical or museological point of view, it is self-evident that our prime interest lies in the evolution of distinctively human forms of behaviour. We are concerned in the end with establishing the identity of man by studying the paleontology of his behaviour and ideology. Prehistoric archaeologists are limited in that they have to depend on fossils, whereas primatologists, social anthropologists, and psychologists are able to confront and in the latter two cases to interrogate living subjects. Yet it is well to remember that those who depend on living witnesses are by this mere fact restricted to an extremely limited range of time. By contrast, prehistorians ought to be able, by means of the disciplines of comparative ethnology, archaeology, and a variety of natural sciences, including animal and in particular primate ethology, to observe the evolution of at least certain aspects of behaviour over the whole span of human existence.

In chapter 2 I sought to argue that the changes in technology and subsistence that allowed man to increase vastly in numbers and extend the range of his settlement into environments more and more distant from those in which the primates evolved were themselves shaped by the same process of natural selection as moulded biological species, even though the precise mechanism by which this operated differed in each case. I concluded that man, so far from making himself, was the product of natural forces, not only in relation to his physique but also in respect to the cultural apparatus by which he was able to achieve his biological dominance; even the most sophisticated products of human ingenuity could be shown to have stemmed in unbroken succession from the sticks, stones, and bones shaped by the earliest man and for that matter from the objects used in still more remote periods by a variety of fossil primates. At the same time I emphasised that even the most primitive industries were the products of human societies—that is, of societies in which behaviour is guided by values that have arisen as a direct result of man's capacity for self-awareness.

One of man's most striking differences from other animals rests in his capacity for objectification. Francisco Romero has described man's uniquely developed "capacity to distinguish objects, to individualise them" as highly cognitive[164] and quite distinct from the merely functional awareness of complexes directly related to vital activities like food winning, reproduction, and self-preservation found among other animals. The manufacture and use of tools—the basic source of archaeological evidence—was in Romero's view only one outcome of man's capacity for objectification: "The successful handling of things presupposes the capacity for objectification. To manipulate things to the degree necessary

[164] Francisco Romero, *Theory of Man*, trans. W. F. Cooper (Berkeley and Los Angeles: University of California Press, 1964), p. 45.

to derive knowledge from their handling presupposes the possibility of discerning them as things, of being aware of their relations, modes and properties."[165]

The capacity for objectification—which in turn made it possible to conceive of symbols, to devise articulate speech, to engage in abstract thought, to practise art, to develop concepts of persons, obligations and values, and to be aware of himself in the context of society—was itself of adaptive value; it improved man's capacity not merely to devise improved apparatus, but to organize it more effectively for social ends in relation to longer periods of time. One could even say that the artificial life of man evolved in the final resort because those with superior powers of objectification were favoured by natural selection at the expense of those with inferior powers. The capacity for objectification depended on the same physical qualities that made possible, and at the same time were favoured adaptively by, the evolution of material culture. Chief among these were stereoscopic vision, relatively unspecialised hands, and above all brains that were not merely larger overall than those of nonhuman primates, but enlarged precisely in the occipital lobe concerned with vision, the temporal and frontal lobes concerned with perception and memory, and "the lower part of the parietal lobe which," to quote Lord Brain, "plays an important part in speech and the use of symbols."[166]

One of the most significant manifestations of man's capacity for objectification has been the development of

[165] *Theory of Man*, p. 18.
[166] Lord Brain, "Science and Behaviour," p. 223.

articulate speech, the means whereby he has been able to classify his environment and social relationships and to fabricate tools for thought and a medium for transmitting and accumulating his cultural heritage. This is hardly a topic that can be directly illuminated by archaeology, but its importance can be made plain by even the most elementary comparison between the means of communication prevalent among the most advanced non-human primates and those of human societies still or until recently living at the most elementary level of economic organisation. Anthropologists have invariably been impressed by the way in which so-called primitive peoples classify their environment in terms of their vocabularies and in relation to their cultural needs.[167] Contrariwise, primatologists agree that the greatest single limitation on the behavioural capacity of the great apes is their entire lack of articulate speech.[168] Of course apes communicate with one another like any other animal. Chimpanzees, for instance, employ a variety of "sounds, gestures, facial and bodily expression, postures

---

[167] The study of how people structure their experience through language is a basic part of the equipment of anthropologists. A good idea of the insight to be gained into the ecological understanding of nonindustrial societies can be had from Donald F. Thomson's description of the Wik-Monkan nomadic hunter-gatherers of Cape York Peninsula in north Queensland in *Proceedings of the Prehistoric Society*, 5 (1939), 212–216.

[168] W. Kohler, in his book *The Mentality of Apes* (London, 1952), concluded that lack of articulate speech together with "a great limitation of those very important components of thought, so-called 'images,' constitute the causes that prevent the chimpanzee from attaining even the smallest beginnings of cultural development" (pp. 227 ff.).

and visible attitudes which function as meaningful signs"; but, apart from "noises of defiance, anger, fear, frustration and contentment,"[169] the nonhuman primates have a notably limited vocabulary.

In the sense that their noises and gestures affect social activities and relations, the great apes certainly have a language; but they have nothing approaching articulate speech. They can convey emotions and desires. Their sounds combined with their bodily movements provide them with a veritable "register of emotional expression," but as Wolfgang Kohler wrote, "it may be taken as positively proved that their gamut of *phonetics* is entirely 'subjective,' and can only express emotions, never designate or describe objects."[170] The language of the nonhuman primates is emotional and affective, whereas human language is capable of being propositional. In each case the linguistic equipment was attuned to the behavioural pattern of the animal concerned. Gestures and emotive signs met the needs of apes behaving in accordance with instinctual patterns. In the case of man the requirements of social life at a cultural level called in addition for articulate speech. Conversely, it may be supposed that every increase in the complexity of material culture and in the level of social integration would

[169] Mrs. Cathy Hayes described the experience of bringing up a chimpanzee from three days to three years. In her book *The Ape in Our House* (New York, 1951), she wrote that after "more than eighteen months of coaching, we have not yet taught Viki to identify her nose, ears, eyes, hands or feet" (p. 29). See also C. F. Hockett and R. Ascher, *Current Anthropology*, 5, no. 3 (1964), 135–163.

[170] *The Mentality of Apes*, pp. 258 ff.

have been accompanied by advances in the potentialities of language. The development of writing[171] and electronic means of communication only mark further steps along the same road. There is a perpetual feedback between the means of communication and the elaboration of culture studied by anthropologists.

If man is a toolmaking animal and one that speaks in an articulate manner, he is also an animal capable of thought. Between speech and thought there is indeed, as the Greeks long ago conveyed in the word λογος, a fundamental identity. Julian Huxley has spelled out the same idea: "True speech involves the use of verbal signs for objects, not merely for feelings. . . . And to have words for objects at once implies conceptual thought"; again, "Words are tools which automatically carve concepts out of experience."[172] Ernst Cassirer has expressed the same point in the context of a child brought up in human society: "by learning to name things a child does not simply add a list of artificial signs to his previous knowledge of ready-made empirical objects. He learns rather to form concepts of those objects, to come to terms with the objective world."[173] If original thought is the rarest commodity in the universe, it is none the less true that the ability to form or at least to react to traditional

[171] For a good discussion of the social implications, see Jack Goody and Ian Watt, "The Consequences of Literacy," *Comparative Studies in Society and History*, 5, no. 3 (1963), 304–345.

[172] Julian Huxley, *The Uniqueness of Man* (London, 1941), p. 3. The immense significance of articulate speech has also been stressed among many others by J. Z. Young in *Doubt and Certainty in Science* (London, 1950), pp. 91, 120.

[173] E. Cassirer, *An Essay on Man* (Yale, 1962), p. 132.

concepts is basic to the functioning of human societies. Again, thought is a basic cause of change: new ideas, ideas which depart from the customary norm, may be compared in their effect with the biological mutations on which the forces of selection operate to produce change. Finally, as men become more fully aware of themselves and their contexts in the world, abstract thought came to play an increasingly active role in the transformation of social life.

Considered as a means of communication, articulate speech must have played as it developed an increasingly important role in facilitating social action in human societies—in societies in which by definition social cohesion was secured at a cultural rather than at a purely instinctive level. Expressed the other way round, one could say that in other forms of animal society there was no need for any other form of communication beyond the emission of the emotive signals needed to release instinctive responses. And since articulate speech would have had no function to perform in such societies, it could hardly have existed. It only became necessary and therefore favoured by selection as cultural life developed; and in its own turn, articulate speech played an immensely important part in the growth of culture. One way in which it did so was by helping to transmit cultural capital, a capital which as it accumulated made even greater demands on language. Whereas instinctive behaviour was to a substantial degree transmitted genetically by built-in drives, the behaviour embodied in culture had to be entirely relearned by each new generation. Although much can be achieved in human as in animal

111

society by direct imitation, every increase in the complexity of culture placed a premium on verbal explanation and precept. In this respect, it is significant that the imparting of verbal traditions is a widespread feature of the ceremonies by which the younger generation is admitted to full adult status even in the simplest surviving societies of man.[174] Gaston Viaud was surely right to maintain that "the real dividing line between man and animals . . . is the possession of conceptual thought and of speech."[175]

If so much is admitted, the question remains how far the prehistorian can document progress in the development of articulate speech from the material at his disposal. The anatomical evidence is, at best, inconclusive. The fact that the areas of the brain cortex concerned with speech are larger in the case of man than in apes is consistent with the idea that the development of speech, as of other aspects of cultural life, affected the evolution of the brain through the adaptive advantage enjoyed by hominids possessed of these attributes. This is not to say that one can draw close inferences from the skulls of early man about their degree of proficiency in speech. There is no anatomical feature—whether jaw shape, mandibular tubercles or endocranial casts—that can of itself be accepted as a valid criterion of speech.[176] On the cultural side the only certain information we have about language

---

[174] Initiation ceremonies are of course much more than occasions for inculcating tribal lore, but this is nevertheless an important function.

[175] Gaston Viaud, *Intelligence: Its Evolution and Forms* (London, 1960), p. 81.

[176] H. V. Vallois in *Social Life of Early Man*, pp. 217–221.

dates from the period of contact with literate civilization. For earlier periods we are left in the realm of mere conjecture. I would only recall in passing Kenneth Oakley's speculation[177] that the marked acceleration in cultural evolution detectable in certain cultures possessed of a lithic technology in mode 4 may have been linked with a breakthrough on the language front, and note the finding of M. Swadesh that "all known languages converge on a monogenetic vanishing point about 40,000 years ago."[178] And significantly enough, as I shall show, the practice of art first appeared in this same context.

The capacity for objectification that made articulate speech and mathematics possible also provided the opportunity for using symbols in many other fields. A common purpose of many of these was to regularise and canalise social behaviour in human societies, in much the same way as the various signals that triggered instinctive patterns of behaviour in nonhuman societies. Symbols of sex, rank, or occupation, for instance, helped to condition the individual for his role in the community. Again, adherence to a given community and difference from neighbouring ones was commonly symbolised by differences of hairstyles, personal ornament, and style and decoration of artifacts in general. Relationships between communities, again, were commonly symbolised by exchanges of material objects that modern observers are liable to interpret as denoting trade.[179] In fact, there are

177 K. P. Oakley, "A Definition of Man," *Science News* (November 20, 1951), p. 75.

178 M. Swadesh, *Southwestern Journal of Anthropology*, 7 (1951), 1–21.

179 See Donald F. Thomson's *Economic Structure and the Cere-*

very few artifacts that could not be interpreted in terms of symbolism.

The first overt sign that men were beginning to be aware of themselves was the formal recognition of death implied by the practice of careful burial. Evidence for this appeared during the late Upper Pleistocene, say around 50 to 60 thousand years ago, over a broad tract of territory from France to Palestine and Uzbekistan. The dead of Neanderthal man were buried in caves, or as in the case of the cemetery at the Mugharet-es-Skhul, Mount Carmel, on a terrace immediately in front of an inhabited cave.[180] Already the practice of flexing the lower limbs by binding them while the body was still limp seems to have been widespread and may indicate an awareness that unless prevented the dead would haunt the living. The precise meaning of the ring of goat skulls set with horns downward round the burial of a child at Teshik-Tash, Uzbekistan[181] (see Fig. 15), may elude us, but it clearly indicates concern with the dead. Advanced Palaeolithic man practiced an even more developed symbolism, covering the dead body with red ochre and placing with it a richer and more regular supply of grave goods.

Among such were commonly included personal ornaments, suggesting that the dead were probably buried

monial Exchange Cycle in Arnhem Land (London, 1949). See also the present writer's "Traffic in Stone Axes and Adze Blades," *Economic History Review*, 18 (1965), 1–28.

[180] See T. D. McCown in D. A. E. Garrod and D. M. A. Bate, *The Stone Age of Mount Carmel*, vol. 1 (Oxford, 1937), chap. 6.

[181] Hallam L. Movius, *Proceedings of the American Philosophical Society*, 97 (1935), 390 ff.

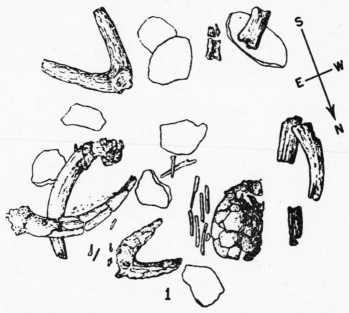

FIG. 15. Mousterian (mode 3) burial at Teshik-Tash *(after Oklad-nikov)*

fully clothed. The practice of ornamenting the person is so general today and ranges so widely among the peoples of the world, from marginal hunter-gatherers to the so-phisticated citizens of the modern metropolis, that it may come as something of a shock to realise how relatively re-cently it appeared in the history of man; for none of the many burials of Neanderthal man has yielded a single indubitable bead or other ornament. When man first began to adorn his person between 30 and 40 thousand years ago, he had taken a further step in personal self-awareness (see Fig. 16). In so doing he sought to achieve by artificial means what nature accomplished through physical attributes. Once men embarked on this course,

FIG. 16. Decorated bracelets: (upper) bronze bracelet decorated in La Tène I style, France *(after British Museum)*; (lower) bracelet of mammoth ivory from the Late Pleistocene of Mezine, South Russia

The Dawn of Self-Awareness

the forces of selection ensured the fantastic proliferation
of cosmetics,[182] mirrors,[183] and jewelry[184] featured in the
archaeology of later periods, not to mention our own

[182] Some of the earliest and fullest evidence for cosmetics comes
from the well-preserved burials of predynastic Egypt. Not only
were stone palettes for grinding pigments among the most characteristic grave goods, but actual materials of the type used for
painting the eyelids have also been found, namely malachite and,
later, galena. Pieces of crude malachite were buried in small linen
or skin bags and powdered malachite has been recovered from
shells, hollow reeds, leaf wrappings and small vases. From the
Middle Kingdom there is good evidence for face painting. See A.
Lucas, *Ancient Egyptian Materials and Industries*, 4th ed. (London, 1962), pp. 80–85.

[183] Reflections in water were presumably the first mirrors. The
earliest artificial ones so far known are the roundels of polished
obsidian from 6th millennium B.C. Çatal Hüyük in Turkey; see
James Mellaart, *Çatal Hüyük* (London, 1967), pp. 79, 208, 211.
Bronze mirrors had already come into use in prehistoric times in
Iran, as at Susa and Sialk III and by the Early Dynastic period in
Sumer (Childe, *New Light on the Most Ancient East* [London,
1952], pp. 137, 149, 196); and they were also present in the Harappan civilization of the Indus Valley (R. E. M. Wheeler, *The Indus
Civilization* [Cambridge, 1962], pl. 21, B). Bronze mirrors were
also used by the Greeks, Etruscans, and Romans as well as by the
barbarian Celts (G. C. Dunning, *Archaeological Journal*, 85 [1930],
69–79) and Scyths. The latter used both handled mirrors, like
those of earlier civilizations, but also looped mirrors of a kind
used by the Chinese from the later Chou dynasty (E. H. Minns,
Scythians and Greeks [Cambridge, 1913], p. 65; William Willetts,
Foundations of Chinese Art [London, 1965], pp. 145–148, figs. 96,
101–104).

[184] See, e.g., R. Vernau, *Les grottes de Grimaldi* (Monaco, 1906),
passim; E. Peters, *Die altsteinzeitliche Kulturstätte Petersfels*
(Augsburg, 1930), pp. 47–50 and pl. 21, 22, 25; E. A. Golomshtok,
The Old Stone Age in European Russia (Philadelphia, 1938), figs.
58–59; B. Klima, *Dolní Věstonice* (Prague, 1963), pls. 68–70.

society. If the admen are right, self-adornment was adaptive in the sense that those most proficient at it were likely to attract the opposite sex. What can be taken for sure is that people have imagined they were making themselves more attractive by painting, combing and generally ornamenting their person, which presupposes that they were sufficiently aware of themselves to go to the trouble they unquestionably did.

It is no accident, but the outcome of the same basic cause, that the first people to ornament themselves were also the first artists. Of music we have only a few simple instruments, whistles and pipes made from phalanges and tubular bones of wild animals;[185] but of representational art we have a plentitude of engravings, paintings, reliefs, and sculptures. Graphic art is a form of symbolizing activity well presented in the archaeological record and one which for the last thirty thousand years or so has most clearly differentiated man from other animals.

Physiologically, there is no reason why the great apes should not have painted pictures. Desmond Morris, in his original and well-illustrated volume, *The Biology of Art*,[186] has shown very clearly that, supplied with suitable equipment, chimpanzees are able to obtain and also convey pleasure by manipulating and juxtaposing pigments. There is no question that apes and monkeys thoroughly enjoy their sessions with paints and brushes. They keenly appreciate the opportunities they afford of an endless variety of rhythmic manipulation. The work of painting seems to be a self-rewarding activity. Any attempt to

[185] J. V. S. Megaw, *Antiquity*, 34 (1960), 16 ff.
[186] London, 1962.

stimulate painting by means of rewards of food is a waste of time. It is equally self-defeating to try to persuade simian painters to continue beyond the limit at which they cease to enjoy it; the most probable outcome is likely to be screams and the destruction of whatever has been achieved. The ape or monkey knows very well when his work is finished; he stops when it has ceased to give him pleasure. To judge from the numbers visiting exhibitions of simian art in London and New York, not to mention the selling prices obtained, it is equally certain that this art is capable of giving pleasure to human observers. Anyone who has looked through the coloured plates of Mr. Morris' book will admit that, if activity and crude colour are admitted as adequate criteria, then the apes and monkeys are capable of producing fine art.

The fact remains that, however well chimpanzees cooperated with Mr. Morris' experiments, they never, left to themselves, produced or even essayed a work of art. Why was this? Surely because they had no ability to symbolize or form images in the imagination. Confirmation of this is available from experiments carried out by a Russian investigator, Mrs. Nadic Kohts, and summarised by Desmond Morris. Mrs. Kohts found that, whereas the scribbles of young children and young apes provided with the same drawing materials may appear very similar, the work they do as they grow older differs in a radical and highly significant way (see Fig. 17). The apes as they matured gained in physical control. On the other hand, it was only the children who went on to form what were clearly images. "No ape, no matter how old or experienced has yet been able to develop graphically to the

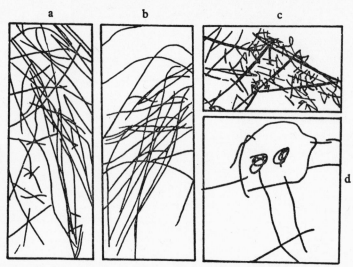

FIG. 17. The graphic capabilities of chimpanzee and human infant: (a, b) early drawings by young chimpanzee Joni (a) and a small boy Roody (b); (c) later drawing by Joni with greater control but no image-making; (d) later drawing by Roody with distinct image *(after Desmond Morris)*

pictorial stage of simple reconstruction," to quote Mr. Morris.[187] The inability of the ape to draw matches his inability to speak. Both reflect an underlying inability to symbolize or form images in the imagination. The point can be illustrated (Pl. I) by reference to the finger-tip scorings *(grabouillage)* on slimey clay on the walls of Altamira.[188] The meaningless macaroni-like marks find a close parallel in the efforts of the chimpanzee; but a representation (Fig. 18) in the same technique of the head of a musk-ox is indisputably "human." [189] As I have already suggested, the practice of graphic art is a com-

[187] *The Biology of Art,* p. 142.
[188] S. Giedion, *The Eternal Present* (London, 1962), fig. 184.
[189] *The Eternal Present,* fig. 188.

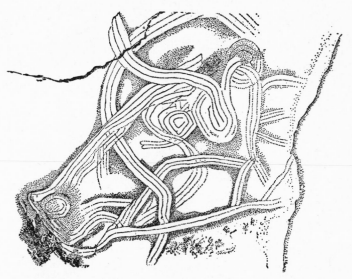

FIG. 18. Outline of bison's head scored in clay at Altamira, North Spain *(after Giedion)*

paratively recent development in the history of mankind. It first appeared in a rudimentary form in the context of the Aurignacian culture in France, that is between *ca.* 33 and 28 thousand B.C., but did not flower until the ensuing Gravettian stage.[190] The practice of art, however one seeks to explain it, implies a capacity not merely to visualise the outer world, but to conceptualise and in a sense to recreate it in the imagination. It is thus a manifestation of an advance in the power of objectification and in the capacity to symbolise the outer world.

Whatever the works of art created by paleolithic man meant to their creators—and on this we can only speculate—they speak to us across the millennia in language

[190] A. Leroi-Gourhan, *Préhistoire de l'art occidental* (Paris, 1965), pp. 38 ff., 242.

much easier for us than for our immediate forefathers to understand. However widely we are separated from Advanced Paleolithic artists by our technology and however much material progress we may have made, we are able to recognise as we contemplate their works that we are in the presence of an art in no way inferior to our own. Let me quote the measured judgement of Herbert Read set out in his lecture on *Art and the Evolution of Man*: "Some of the painters of Greek vases, some of the medieval illuminators of manuscripts, the great painters of the Renaissance, certain painters of the 19th century—all these have perhaps reached the level of aesthetic quality present in the cave paintings of Lascaux or Altamira, but they have not exceeded that original standard."[191]

It is a striking fact that among the first people to recognise this in our modern world were the artists who broke through the crust of nineteenth century academicism, counterpart of the Western dominated worldview attacked by Arnold Toynbee. Historians of modern art—or of what until recently was accepted as such—are agreed on the significance of the influence exerted by prehistoric and ethnographic arts on the painters and sculptors of western Europe during the first half of the twentieth century.[192] We have it on the authority of

[191] *Art and the Evolution of Man* (London, 1951), p. 12.

[192] The impact of Negro and Pacific art on the Cubist and Expressionist movement in the early twentieth-century European art is sufficiently well known; e.g., E. Langui, *Fifty Years of Modern Art* (London, 1959), pp. 21, 31. The English sculptor Jacob Epstein, who like many of his contemporary artists collected primitive art, devoted a chapter in *Epstein: An Autobiography* (London, 1955) to "African and Polynesian Carvings, and Mask of Nefer-

PLATE I
Doodling in clay and paint by early man and chimpanzee:
(above) on the cave wall at Altamira, North Spain *(after Giedion);*
(below) on board by chimpanzee Betsy *(after Desmond Morris)*

PLATE II
Ivory carving from Brassempouy, France

PLATE III
Stone carvings of the female form, ancient
and modern: *(left)* from the Paleolithic site of Kostienki,
South Russia *(ca.* 15 cm.); *(right)* by the modern
French sculptor Dodeigne *(ca.* 157 cm.)

PLATE IV

The female form, ancient and modern:
(*left and middle*) front and back of a 5-cm. carving
in haematite from Ostrava-Petřkovice, Czechoslovakia;
(*right*) bronze relief "The Back II" by Henri Matisse
(*photo, the Tate Gallery, London*)

Henry Moore that he treated the galleries of the British Museum as his university. And Moore tells us specifically how he was drawn to the Venus of Brassempouy (Pl. II) "a lovely tender carving of a girl's head no bigger than one's thumbnail."[193] Again, it is no less interesting to observe how sculptors, once freed from the insistent need to perpetuate the academic tradition stemming from the Classical world by way of the Renaissance, have expressed themselves in an idiom sometimes astonishingly like that of their prehistoric forebears. To some extent, no doubt, this is a matter of more or less direct influence through illustrations but not, I believe, wholly so. I will content myself by citing a marble carving by the French sculptor Dodeigne and ask you to compare it with a much smaller one carved in soft stone (Pl. III) from the Paleolithic site of Kostienki I in South Russia.[194] It is most unlikely that in this case we have direct influence, since the Kostienki illustration was not yet available in readily accessible books. I think we must accept that confronted

---

titi." Epstein notes explicitly that "it was the artists who first saw the sculptural qualities of African work" and maintains that this "opens up to us a world hitherto unknown . . ." (p. 188). Henry Moore's B.B.C. lecture of 1941, now reprinted in *Henry Moore on Sculpture* (ed. Philip James [London, 1966], pp. 155–163) betrays the sculptor's interest in a wide range of primitive art; the impact of early Mexican art on certain of his stone carvings is evident. A particularly fine collection of small African wooden carvings has been formed by the Polish-born artist, Josef Herman, who for many years has worked in Britain; here again, the affinity can be seen in many of the figures in his paintings.

[193] "Primitive Art," *Listener* (April 24, 1941), pp. 598 ff.

[194] E. A. Golomshtok, *The Old Stone Age*, pl. 21; P. P. Efimenko, *Kostienki I* (Moscow, 1959), pl. 18.

with a human torso or head the modern, nonacademic artist reacts in the same way as his forebear of ten or twenty thousand years ago. Perhaps we can usefully consider the matter the other way round. Facts such as those I have cited confirm us in our view that Paleolithic man had already attained the ability to express in symbolic form what he felt about the human body or the wild animals on which he so largely depended, and in doing so produced works of art in no demonstrable way inferior to those of contemporary artists in Western civilization.

Another field of awareness in which man is uniquely perceptive is that of time. All organisms regulate their daily and seasonal routines by means of what may be termed physiological clocks activated in the main by changes in the intensity and duration of light. Man is subject to the same organic regulators; but as he has become aware of time he has devised cultural means to supplement physiological time, just as in communication he has reinforced gestures by speech. In doing so, he has improved his biological effectiveness by extending the depth and range of his self-awareness. He has effectively added a new dimension to his life. To realise that he exists in time is one way in which a man experiences his difference from a nonhuman primate.

Observers of apes and monkeys agree that their highly restricted appreciation of past and future time is, along with their lack of articulate speech, one of their gravest limitations. Gaston Viaud has said of the chimpanzees that they "are more or less trapped in the present."[195]

---

[195] *Intelligence*, p. 80.

The Dawn of Self-Awareness

There seems, indeed, to be a close link between a restricted awareness of time and lack of articulate speech. From his work on macaque monkeys John Coles concluded that their "mental activities and processes . . . are limited almost entirely to the present. Even when they are related to past experience, or refer to a very limited and immediate future, they appear always to be linked to sensory stimuli in the environmental present."[196] A point to emphasise is that Coles associates this temporal limitation with the fact that macaques communicate primarily by vision and touch. They possess the organs for vocalisation, but they only developed them to a rudimentary degree, mainly because they live almost entirely in the sensory present. They were under no pressure to develop verbalisation because they had no occasion to converse about the past or plan for the future.

The converse is true of man. As Gaston Viaud has put it, "the reconstruction of the past is only possible because we have speech and conceptual thought, together with habits and social understanding. In fact, we recall the past by word-associations."[197] "Words, said Bergson, are the carriers of memory."[198] Like other animals, men

[196] John Coles in John Napier and N. A. Barnicot (ed.), *The Primates* (Symposia of the Zoological Society of London, No. 10, London, 1963), p. iii.

[197] Viaud, *Intelligence*, p. 82.

[198] A. Irving Hallowell, "Temporal Orientation in Western Civilization and in Preliterate Society," *American Anthropologist*, 39 (1937), 647–670; E. Evans-Pritchard, *The Nuer* (Oxford, 1940), p. 103; Raymond Firth, *We, the Tikopia* (London, 1936), pp. 97 ff.; A. R. Brown, *The Andaman Islanders* (Cambridge, 1922), pp. 119 and 311 ff.

experience the promptings of physiological time, but unlike them they show themselves to be aware of time by naming segments of it and, in due course, by measuring it. In general, it seems that peoples living at an elementary level of technology divided time in relation to their economic needs. Thus, the Wik Monkan people of Cape York, Queensland, distinguish five seasons with differing patterns of weather, plant life, subsistence, technology, and settlement.[199] It was not until the development of machine-based industry that punctuality and the precise measurement of time became strictly necessary for economic reasons. But in matters of time, as in so many other aspects of existence, men have not been activated by purely economic motives. Exploration of the environment, for instance, is as basic a drive in men as in rats. Indeed, one might almost say that man, dependent for almost the whole of his existence on assessing the qualities and habits of a wide range of animals and plants, has been selected basically for his powers of precise observation: it was the best applied ecologists who were most likely to leave posterity and therefore to survive.

Yet there is no reason to suppose that men have confined their observation to aspects of their environment of immediate use to them. On the contrary, we know that exploration is a basic drive independent of the quest for food. As men's powers of objectification and articulate speech developed, so it may be supposed did their ability to speculate on what they saw. It is no wonder that the night sky or the behaviour of the sun and the moon

[199] Donald F. Thomson, "The Seasonal Factor in Human Culture," *Proceedings of the Prehistoric Society*, 5 (1939), 209–221.

should have attracted the attention of primitive man. The Bushmen, for instance, do not merely observe closely the phases of the moon and divide the day according to the position of the sun, but some of them foretell seasonal change from the stars; the Naron, we are told, accept the heliacal rising (i.e., the last rising before dawn) of the Pleiades as a herald of the cold season.[200] Since for all practical purposes the Bushmen, and indeed all peoples still outside the range of industrial society, rely on direct observation of the weather and of changes in animal and plant life, one may ask why they should worry about the stars or the planets. Clearly this is not for economic reasons. But there is, after all, no reason why man's curiosity should be restricted to matters of strict utility any more than the curiosity of a cow or a dog; and unlike these domestic animals he is equipped to seek to explain what he observes. If one asks why he should want an explanation, one answer might be that he does so in order to meet the apprehensions that accompany self-awareness. The price of knowledge is anxiety or at least an awareness of ignorance. Is not this the nemesis of education? The more we have of it, the more keenly we are or ought to be aware of our ignorance. Yet it is precisely because of this awareness that we feel the need to know more by asking questions and by seeking to understand what we observe. The thirst for knowledge is a direct outcome of self-awareness. And of all the mysteries that confronted man as he emerged from the womb of instinctive life into the world of self-awareness and culture,

200 I. Schapera, *The Khoisian Peoples of South Africa* (London, 1930), pp. 217 ff.

none can have been more frightening or more poignant than the mystery of time.

What hard evidence have we that prehistoric man in fact concerned himself with time beyond the needs of his daily life? As always in dealing with the past we can only proceed on hypothesis. It is a merit of Alexander Marshack that by the painstaking analysis of incisions, often minute, on ivory and bone artifacts of Advanced Paleolithic men he has drawn attention to series of marks that can hardly be accidental and yet do not in many cases conform to decorative designs.[201] Until Mr. Marshack's results are published in much more detail, his preliminary findings have naturally to be taken with reserve; but it does begin to look as though he has disclosed the existence of a form of notation. In certain instances, indeed, this appears to be reasonably consistent with systematic observation of the moon, as one can see by comparing a drawing of the incisions cut on a mammoth[202] bone from a late glacial site at Gontzi, South Russia, dating from approximately ten thousand years B. C. with Mr. Marshack's exegesis in terms of four cycles in the waxing and waning of the moon.

In the case of early settled communities, preoccupation with time often took a monumental form. The ceremonial centers erected by the Maya in Guatemala and eastern Mexico were laid out, like the famous one at Uaxactún (see Fig. 19), so that the sun might be ob-

---

[201] "Lunar Notation on Upper Palaeolithic Remains," *Science*, 146, no. 3645 (November 6, 1964), 743–745.

[202] *Science*, vol. 146, fig. 2. For another drawing of the same piece of engraved ivory, see E. A. Golomshtok, *The Old Stone Age*, fig. 75.

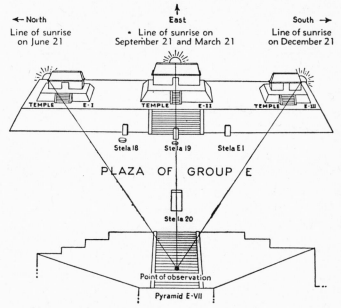

FIG. 19. Astronomical planning of Maya structures at Uaxactun, Guatemala *(after Morley)*

served to rise at solstices and equinoxes over key points.[203] In addition, special observatories were built like the round tower at Chichen Itza,[204] its wall apertures precisely designed to give sightings from a central chamber on the north-south declinations of the moon and the setting of the sun at the spring equinox. Scholars have indeed amply confirmed the accuracy of the Maya astronomers.[205] To quote only a few of their achievements, the Mayas, whose technology was still a Stone Age one, calculated the duration of the solar year more accurately than the framers of the Julian or even the Gregorian cal-

[203] S. G. Morley, *The Ancient Maya*, 3rd ed., rev. George W. Brainerd (Stanford, 1956), fig. 33.
[204] *The Ancient Maya*, fig. 28.
[205] *The Ancient Maya*, p. 256.

endars; without fractions they nevertheless got extremely close to the modern determination of the lunar month; and the priests prepared tables of eclipses so accurate that they were able to base their power on their ability to predict and so in a sense control happenings that would otherwise have been terrifying. The Mayas were obsessed with calendars because they desired above all to ensure that the wheel of time continued to revolve. Study of the inscriptions on the monuments themselves, together with those preserved in the surviving codices, shows that the priests kept two distinct years. For regulating their religious ceremonies, they followed sacred years each comprising 13 uinals of 20 days; whereas for civil purposes, they adhered to years of 18 uinals plus 5 days and an occasional correction. By combining the two, the Maya arrived at the concept of what they devoutly hoped would be an endless cycle of Calendar Rounds, each equivalent to 52 civil and 73 sacred years. And beyond this they constructed a heirarchy of units ascending by vigesimal multiplication from the basic *tun* of 360 to the preposterous *aluntun* of some 23,040 million days. Plainly, these hypothetical units served a psycho-religious rather than a strictly economic purpose. Above all, they were designed to assuage the haunting anxiety that time might one day end.

For some years[206] it has been widely accepted that Stonehenge, perhaps the most famous prehistoric monument in Europe, was laid out on an astronomical basis. This has been strongly reinforced by Gerald Hawkins'

[206] Since the publication in 1906 of Sir Norman Lockyer's *Stonehenge and Other British Stone Monuments Astronomically Considered.*

analysis[207] of the precise setting of such features as pits and stone uprights, which makes it seem extremely probable that the people who laid out the monument paid careful attention to the behaviour of the moon as well as of the sun. (see Figs. 20 and 21). It is not necessary to follow Hawkins all the way to agree that at each stage in its history the monument was planned in relation to significant positions of the moon as well as of the sun. Again, the correspondence between the numbers of component elements and such astronomical factors as the number of days in the lunar month or the number of years involved in the periodic swing of the moon is hardly likely to be a mere coincidence. The frequent reconstruction of the monument suggests a concern of long standing and argues for transmission through some institution, whether a corporation or a kinship group. The mere labour involved in transporting, erecting and reerecting large stones from at least three sources[208] again argues for some overriding concern and interest maintained over considerable periods of time and directed by some central authority. The suggestion is strong that this concern centered on the movements of the heavenly bodies. It could well be that the directing authority was a kind of priesthood whose prestige and authority stemmed from its ability, using the monument as a kind of observatory, to predict such events as eclipses.

Other examples of monuments almost certainly laid out in connection with astronomical observations can be quoted from central Europe. One might, for instance,

[207] Gerald S. Hawkins, *Stonehenge Decoded* (New York, 1965; London, 1966).

[208] R. J. C. Atkinson, *Stonehenge* (London, 1956).

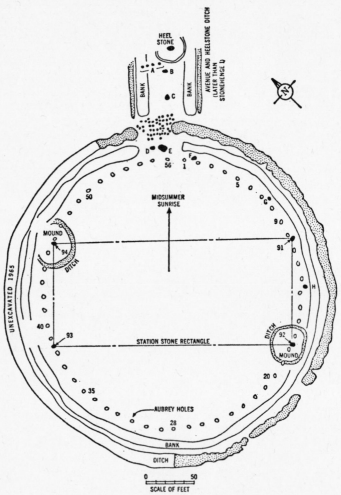

FIG. 20. Plan of Stonehenge I *(after Hawkins)*

mention the two concentric stone settings enclosing a
D-shaped setting at Sarmigetuza, Rumania, described by
C. Daicoviciu[209] as a calendrical monument set up by

[209] *Dacia IV* (1960), 231–254; cf. *Bulletin de la Société Préhistorique Française*, 60 (1963), 408–410.

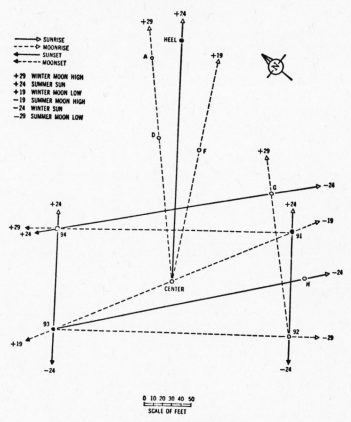

FIG. 21. Diagram showing principal alignments at Stonehenge I, each directed to some significant position of the sun or the moon *(after Hawkins)*

the Dacians and slighted by the Romans like Stonehenge; or, again, there is the oblong monument at Libenice, Kolin, Czechoslovakia, claimed[210] to be orientated in relation to the rising of the sun.

Another uniquely human manifestation of self-aware-

---

[210] Jan Filip, *Enzyklopädisches Handbuch zur Ur- und Frühgeschichte Europas*, (2 vols., Prague, 1966 and 1969), p. 708.

ness to appear, however incompletely and opaquely in the archaeological record, is the expression of religious feeling that stems in the final resort from a sense of personal insignificance in the face of powerful but imperfectly understood forces external to the organism. Anxiety extending far beyond the immediate apprehensions common to other animals and permeating every aspect of experience is an inevitable accompaniment of self-awareness. It was only as men began to appreciate their predicament, the dangers that menaced their survival, and the prospect at no very distant date of their own personal deaths that they became a prey to long-term anxiety. And if they were to continue to operate as effective organisms it was essential for them to find some way of relieving these anxieties. One way of achieving this was to acquire knowledge of cause and effect and a progressive increase in such knowledge is precisely what the development of material culture has been about. Yet it is a fallacy to imagine that the growth of knowledge necessarily reduces the area of uncertainty. The contrary might be argued. Even at an intellectual level the main result of extending knowledge is paradoxically to increase the area or at least the awareness of ignorance. This fact, that the more we know the more we know what we don't know, is surely the key to the exponential growth in the expansion of knowledge, most strikingly shown today in the sphere of natural science. It is even open to discussion whether prehistoric man was as an individual less ignorant than modern man, since advances in knowledge have been achieved by specialisa-

tion, that is on narrow fronts. In modern societies the
fragmentation of knowledge has to some extent been
overcome by philosophic systems, but such are as a rule
comprehensible only to comparatively few persons.

For most men and for all preliterate men, the need
could only be met by a combination of myths, ritual,
magic, and worship. Of the rituals that served to lessen
the anxieties of passing from one phase of existence to
another, none were more solemn than those that centered round the fact of death. It is no surprise that it was
in the practice of careful burial that early man left the
first tangible memorial of his growing sense of self-
awareness; nor again that so many of the outstanding
monuments of subsequent ages should have been tombs
and their furnishings; whether one has in mind the
elaborate masonry structures of advanced civilizations
or the hardly less various ones erected by preliterate societies. Of the former, the Pyramids of Old Kingdom
Egypt are outstanding, not merely for their scale but
even more for their precision. The Great Pyramid was
not only enormous by any standards—some 756 feet
square at the base and 481 feet high, it was made of about
2,300,000 blocks of around 2.5 tons each—but it was built
to narrow standards of accuracy and incorporated an intricate series of chambers and corridors. Sir Flinders
Petrie estimated that a hundred thousand men may
have been conscripted to transport the stone blocks and
that the actual construction of the pyramid might have
involved a permanent work force of perhaps forty thousand men; for a whole series of monuments of this type

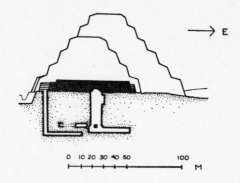

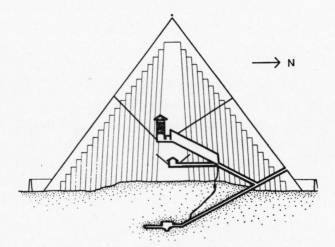

FIG. 22. Egyptian pyramids of the Old Kingdom: (upper) stepped pyramid at Sakkara and (lower) great pyramid at Gizeh *(after Aldred)*

(see Fig. 22) was constructed to house the dead rulers of the Old Kingdom.[211] Despite their massive scale and intricate internal arrangements, the pyramid burials were robbed in antiquity. Some idea of the wealth of pharaonic burials is, however, afforded by the discovery of the

[211] I. E. S. Edwards, *The Pyramids of Egypt* (London, 1961).

robbed but still substantially intact burial of Tutankhamen, one of the last rulers of the Eighteenth Dynasty,
the finds from which are today one of the main tourist at-
tractions of Egypt.[212] The excavation by Leonard Woolley of the tombs of the kings of the First Dynasty of Ur
provide an additional insight into the burial ritual of
one of the great civilizations of antiquity, because apart
from the wealth and diversity of the material goods deposited with the royal dead, there were the skeletons of
his retinue sacrificed to accompany their lord into the
next world.[213] In proportion to their wealth the preliterate peoples of many parts of the world, more particularly those whose economies were based to any extent on
stock-raising or farming, constructed funerary monuments and in some cases deposited grave goods of a comparable degree of size and richness. This applies whether
we turn to the megalithic chamber tombs of the Mediterranean and Atlantic litorals[214] and of Japan,[215] or to
the earthen burial mounds of Eurasia[216] and the eastern
United States of America.[217] Of the many other forms of

[212] Howard Carter and A. C. Mace, *The Tomb of Tutankhamen*
(London, 1923–1933).

[213] C. L. Woolley, *Ur Excavations*; vol. 2, *The Royal Cemetery*
(London, 1938).

[214] For an introduction, see Glyn Daniel, *The Megalith Builders
of Western Europe* (London, 1938).

[215] For accessible illustrations of protohistoric megalithic tombs
in Japan, see J. E. Kidder, *Japan Before Buddhism* (London, 1959),
fig. 35 and pls. 69–71.

[216] V. G. Childe, *The Dawn of European Civilization*, 6th ed.
(London, 1957), *passim*.

[217] James B. Griffin, *Archaeology of Eastern United States* (Chicago, 1952), pp. 93, 202 ff., 357.

ritual that served to ease the activities of everyday life, reduce tension, and contribute to social solidarity, archaeology furnishes only enigmatic clues. Yet it is plain that ritual activities as a conspicuous feature of peculiarly human behaviour must have grown up in prehistoric times; they were selected in the evolution of human behaviour because they served a vital function.

The importance of myths and legends as media for reassuring men as they became aware of time and the role they played in both strengthening social solidarity and in differentiating one community from another has already been touched on in the first chapter (pp. 41–45). For obvious reasons we have no direct evidence for these from the preliterate societies of the remote past, but the record from the recent ethnographic past is a full one[218] and goes far to suggest the importance of this means of validating the surroundings and existing customs of individual societies.

Magic—the belief that by going through the correct motions it was possible, so to say, to appropriate something of the power or mana inherent in living things, springs, or material objects—is widespread among unsophisticated men today and there are many hints in the archaeological record that it was widely shared in the prehistoric past. Although no longer accepted as the sole key to Paleolithic art, there can hardly be any doubt that magic was an element in this manifestation of pre-

[218] See B. Malinowski, "Myth in Primitive Psychology," *The Fraser Lecture, 1922–1932*, ed. W. R. Dawson (London, 1932), pp. 66–119; A. R. Brown, *The Andaman Islanders* (London, 1922), chap. 4.

historic mentality; the jab marks on the clay body of the
bear in the Grotte de Montespan, for instance, can hardly admit of any other explanation.[219] Magical ideas can
be seen embodied in some of the beads and amulets[220]
that men have worn these thirty or forty thousand years.
Or one might point to the veneration of springs, certainly
attested as far back as the Bronze Age in Europe in the
tangible form of the bronzes deposited in the spring of
St. Moritz.[221] One might also cite the practice of trepanning the skull to allow the escape of evil spirits.[222] Although, so long as they were believed in, the efficacy
of magical practices was in no way affected by their
biological validity, it is interesting that each of the
last two practices was, in fact, soundly based on physical
reality; trepannation is still practised by surgeons to re-
lieve local conditions of the brain that might in primitive
society have been attributed to evil spirits, and the cha-
lybeate in the springs of St. Moritz have caused them to
be sought for cures down to modern times.

[219] S. Giedion, *The Eternal Present*, p. 182; A. Leroi-Gourhan,
Préhistoire, p. 123 f.

[220] The use of certain types of shell, even if these had to be obtained from a great distance, as with the case of the *Spondylus
gaederopus* ornaments found in later Danubian I burials over a
large part of middle Europe, is a case in point; see the present
author's *Prehistoric Europe: The Economic Basis* (London, 1952),
p. 241 ff.

[221] J. Heierli, "Die bronzezeitliche Quellfassung von St. Moritz,"
Anz. f. Schweizerische Altertumskunde, n.s. vol. 9 (1907), 4 hft.,
265–278. See also *Antiquity*, 18 (1944), 5.

[222] Stuart Piggot, "A Trepanned Skull of the Beaker Period
from Dorset and the Practice of Trepanning in Prehistoric Europe," *Proceedings of the Prehistoric Society*, 6 (1940), 112–132.

The veneration of powers immanent in living beings, the heavenly bodies,[223] thunder,[224] springs, and material objects is surely the source of religious feeling even if veneration was in time transferred to a pantheon of anthropomorphic deities and ultimately brought to converge on the notion of a supreme being. The animals and generative forces depicted or symbolised in designs on the walls and roofs of the paleolithic caves of Western Europe must surely stand in a relation to religion analogous to that of the carvings, paintings, and frescoes in a Christian church. Between the two, an immense evolution has of course occurred, not only in the object of worship, but no less in the manner of its organisation; yet the analogy lies across a thousand generations and the barriers of huge steps in social evolution.

The archaeological record makes it possible to follow

[223] The importance of the sun in the mythology of the Teutonic Bronze Age is richly documented, e.g. by the famous Trundholm sun car with its gold-plated disc supported on wheels drawn by a horse (J. Brøndsted, *Danmarks Oldtid*, 2:85–88), by bronze amulets with amber disc inset (*ibid.*, p. 145), and by representations on the Swedish rock engravings (*ibid.*, p. 144).

[224] In the folklore not merely of Europe, but of large parts of Asia and Africa, stone axes featured as thunderbolts; Sir John Evans, *Ancient Stone Implements of Great Britain* (London, 1897), pp. 56–60. The cult of the double axe in Minoan Crete must surely be related to the same idea; see *A Companion to Homer*, eds. A. J. B. Wace and Frank H. Stubbings (London, 1962), p. 465. The practice of placing a stone axe under the rafters or in the foundations of a house as a protection against lightning, known among recent European peasants, was apparently practiced, at least as regards foundations, by the Middle Neolithic peasants of Denmark; see J. Winther, *Troldebjerg* (Rudkjøbing, 1935), fig. 53.

in some detail the elaboration at least of the architectural setting of public, institutionalised religion. The ancient Sumerians, for example, spent so much of their resources in the frequent rebuilding and elaboration of temples and auxiliary structures that archaeologists have rightly concentrated on these as the best keys to the unfolding of Mesopotamian protohistory. No less than thirteen successive temple structures could be recognised in the Ubaid levels at Abu Shahrain, and the key to the Uruk sequence at the eponymous site (Fig. 23) was found in the successive reconstructions of the Eanna and later the Anu temples.[225] The progressive developments from the single squarish cell plan in the lowest level at Abu Shahrain to the monumental tripartite White Temples built at the culmination of the Uruk phase and set on a great rectangular mud-brick platform some 13 metres high and 70 by 66 metres in plan, reflects not only the growth in the social surplus of Sumerian societies, but also the degree to which this was concentrated on the service of the gods and of their servitors. Or, again, to choose an example from the New World, one might point to the elaboration of ceremonial centres that appeared already in the Formative but which reached their climax in the Classic phase of Mesoamerican civilization.[226] The most prominent feature of these, if we except their sheer scale and the majesty of planning on such a site as Teotihuacán, are the stepped pyramidal

[225] V. Gordon Childe, *New Light on the Most Ancient East* (London, 1952), p. 12.

[226] Gordon R. Willey, *An Introduction to American Archaeology* (Englewood Cliffs, New Jersey, 1966), 1:117.

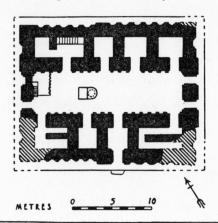

FIG. 23. The White Temple at Uruk, Mesopotamia, fourth millennium B.C. *(after Childe)*

temple structures rising to heights of 60 meters or more at sites like Tikal, Capán, Uaxactún, faced with masonry and crowned by massive temples adorned with elaborate stone carving and stucco ornament.

By any standards the temple structures set up by the Sumerians or the Maya were substantial, but it is only when one considers the technical poverty of their builders—the Maya, for instance, had no metal tools, no effective draught animals, and no wheels—and the relatively humble nature of their private dwellings that one appreciates fully the significance of their social roles. One is struck, as forcibly as one is struck when contemplating a great Christian cathedral, such as that rising amid the lowly huddle of buildings that even today constitutes the City of Ely in eastern England, by the compelling nature of the need that drove men to build structures so immense and so richly embellished. It is ironical that archaeology should be so highly prized by votaries of the materialist interpretation of history, when so few of the outstanding monuments or even of the finest artifacts revealed by excavation can, in fact, be explained in material terms.

The overriding characteristic of man, as distinct from other primates, manifests itself in the mere process of self-awareness. Other animals, as we come to know them closely, may be seen to exhibit traits of appearance and behaviour that mark them off, even if only slightly, from other members of the same species. To this extent they may be said to possess individual features. Yet, except in the imagination of human observers, they are not persons. The only beings who can be considered persons are those capable of articulate speech and thought, of aesthetic appreciation, of realising and assessing their context in time and place, and of appreciating the existence of powers outside themselves and ultimately of imagining deity—beings moreover able to exercise conscious discrimination and choice and open to a sense of moral obligation to others, in other words men. Yet even this supreme attribute of men was, as I have argued (p. 107), of adaptive value; as human personality developed, so did thought and conscious choice, and so therefore did the range of deviation on which natural selection was able to play. There is, thus, an evident link between the degree of humanisation and the rate of cultural change.

Yet, conversely, the more important human personality became as a factor in the evolutionary process, the more necessary became social rules, since the continuity of culture depended less on individuals than on the moral communities which made them human. Whereas among animals social groups were held together by instinctive drives and patterns of behaviour, among men, because of the fact of self-awareness, it was necessary to formalise interpersonal relationships within social groups: among all men, at whatever level of development we can observe today, social obligations are defined by custom and stabilised by religious or equivalent sets of values. Man's behaviour, even at the most elementary biological level, is regulated by socially inherited rules and operates through (or in opposition to) established institutions, a fact which redeems from absurdity the famous contention of Lévi-Strauss that the prohibition of incest is not only the precondition of culture, but in effect is culture.[227] Indeed, when one contemplates human behaviour, one is hard put, in the words of Julian Huxley, "to find any human activities which are not

[227] Claude Lévi-Strauss, *The Elementary Structures of Kinship*, ed. Rodney Needham (London, 1969).

unique."[228] Even the most basic biological functions—such as eating, sheltering, pairing and breeding, fighting, and dying—are performed in idioms acquired by belonging to historically and locally defined cultural groups whose patterns of behaviour are conditioned by particular sets of values. One does not surely have to accept Teilhard de Chardin's noosphere[229] to appreciate that man is indeed a very special kind of animal. He has become such a special animal by a process of evolution in the course of prehistory.

In chapter 2 I maintained that the material progress that enabled man to multiply, to occupy almost all environments, to dominate other animals, and to evolve a new form of social life was a product of the same forces of selection as those that moulded other forms of life. I see no reason why we need treat man's conceptual life or social institutions in any other way. If these are unique to man, they are no more so than the machine tools and atomic reactors that have developed by the insensible degrees attested by archaeology from the most primitive artifacts. They are equally the result of replacing or at least controlling instinctive patterns of behaviour by ones shaped by culture and made actual to individuals through the growth of self-awareness. In the new culturally orientated way of life one can say that the distinctively human abilities and qualities, such as articulate speech, conceptual thought, the practice of art, the assessment of time, personality, awareness of social obligations

[228] *Evolution as a Process*, p. 29.
[229] *The Phenomenon of Man*.

and ties, and religious observance were, in a broad sense, adaptive. Societies of human character have been better fitted for survival in a cultural milieu precisely to the extent that they are human; and the record of archaeology testifies over the last few tens of thousands of generations to an increasingly human pattern of behaviour.

Index

Abu Shahrain, Iraq, temple of Ubaid culture, 141

Academia Sinica, 24

Acculturation, 67, 68

Afontova Gora II, Siberia, 76 n.

African prehistory: European contribution, 29–31; earliest stone industries (mode 1), 70; earliest bifaces (mode 2), 71, 72; iron metallurgy, 82

Agriculture, 78, 88, 89. *See also* Cereal crops; Farming; Reaping knives

Alaska, 77

Albright, W. F., American archaeologist, 20 n.

Ali Kosh, Iran, American excavations, 22

Altamira, Spain: *grabouillage* (scoring) on clay walls, 120; paintings, 122

Al'Ubaid, Iraq: British excavations, 22; culture, 141

Anati, E., Italian prehistorian, 78 n.

Anderson, J. G., Swedish pioneer of Chinese prehistory, 24

Index

Black, Davidson, discoverer of Pekin man, 24

Blegen, Carl, American archaeologist, 35 n.

Boats, sea-going, 79, 83

Bones, animal, utilized as tools, 65

Boule, M., French paleontologist, 26 n.

Bowker, Thomas Holden, 28

Braidwood, Robert, American prehistorian, 22, 86

Brain, 58, 59, 107, 112

Brain, Lord, 107

Brassempouy, France: Venus head carving, 123

Breuil, Henri, French prehistorian: researches in China, 24; system, 26; travels, 33, 34; on early use of bone, 65 n.

British archaeology overseas: institutes and schools, 16 n.; Greece, 18, 19; Egypt, 19, 20; southwest Asia, 21–23; India, 23, 29

Brockman-Jerosch, H., Swiss botanist, 89 n.

Brondsted, J., Danish archaeologist, 140 n.

Brown, A. R., British social anthropologist, 125 n., 138 n.

Buckland, Dean, pioneer British cave excavator, 9, 10, 13

Buffon, Georges, French naturalist, 12

Buret', Siberia, paleolithic house, 90 n.

Burial, first overt sign of self-awareness, 114, 115, 135–137

Burkitt, M. C., British prehistorian, 26 n.

Bushman, South African: ob-

servation of sun, moon, and stars, 127

Butterfield, H., British historian, 46 n.

Butzer, Karl W., paleontologist, 36 n.

California, University of (Berkeley), 34

Camden, William, English antiquary, 6, 7

Campbell, Bernard, British physical anthropologist, 57 n., 63

Can Hasan, Turkey, British excavations, 23

Cann, J. R., British mineralogist, 80 n., 81

Capán, Maya centre, 142

Carmel, Mount, caves, 20, 21

Carter, Howard, British Egyptologist, 137

Cassirer, Ernst, American philosopher, 110

Çatal Hüyük, Turkey, British excavations, 23

Caton-Thompson, G., British prehistorian, excavations in Egypt, 20 n., 78 n., 94 n.

Cereal crops, 93–95

Ceremonial centres, Maya, 141

Chadwick, John, 18

Chappell, J., New Zealand, petrologist, 80 n.

Chardin, Teilhard de, French prehistorian and philosopher, 24, 145

Cheng Te-k'un, sinologue, 6 n., 78 n.

Chicago University, Oriental Institute, 34

149

Index

Index

Index

prehistorians, 31, 70 n., 84
Lehringen, Saxony, Germany, wooden spear, 65 n., 66
Leroi-Gourhan, A., French prehistorian, 121 n., 139 n.
Lévi-Strauss, Claude, French social anthropologist, 144
Lhwyd, Edward, Welsh antiquary, 13
Libby, Willard F., inventor of radiocarbon analysis, 38
Libenice, Kolin, Czechoslovakia, monument orientated to rising sun, 133
Literacy and historical awareness, 42, 59, 60. See also Scripts; Writing
Lockyer, Norman, British astronomer, 130 n.
Lubbock, John, British pioneer of prehistory, 5 n., 14, 15, 87
Luther, Martin, 10
Lyell, Charles, British geologist, 11, 12

McBryde, Isabel, Australian prehistorian, 80 n.
McBurney, C. B. M., British prehistorian, 69 n., 72 n.
McCown, T. D., American physical anthropologist, 114
MacCurdy, Grant, American prehistorian, 35 n.
MacNeish, R. S., American prehistorian: subsistence in Mesoamerica, 86, 93
Magic, 135, 138, 139
Maize, wild and cultivated, 92, 93
Makapansgat, South Africa, 65
Malinowski, B., British social anthropologist, 138 n.

Mal'ta, Siberia, palaeolithic site, 75 n., 90 n.
Man: an animal conditioned by culture, 50, 52; physical evolution, 56, 107; a domesticated animal, 64. See also Humanity; Self-awareness
Mangelsdorf, P. C., American geneticist, 93
Maps, 42
Marshack, Alexander, American science writer, 128
Masson, V., Russian prehistorian, 22 n.
Material culture: means of supplementing limbs, 55–57
Materialist interpretation of history, 32; inadequacy of, 143
Materials, raw: taking into use of more effective, 13, 79; traffic in, 80, 81
Mathematical thought: associated with idea of fixed order of nature, 10, 11; Maya, 130
Maya civilization: lack of metallurgy, 82; ceremonial centres, 128–130, 141–143; calendars and observatories, 129
Megalithic chamber tombs, 137
Megaw, J. V. S., British prehistorian, 118 n.
Meldgaard, J., Danish archaeologist, 22 n.
Mellaart, James, British archaeologist, 23, 78 n., 117 n.
Menghin, Oswald, Austrian prehistorian, 5 n.
Mersin, Turkey, British excavations, 23
Metallurgy: modes, 68; social implications, 80; native cop-

Aspects of Prehistory

per, 81; bronze metallurgy, 81, 82; iron, 82

Mexico, 92, 93, 128–130, 141

Mezine, south Russia, mammoth ivory bracelet, 116

Microlithic industries (mode 5), 76, 77

Miles, S. W., American anthropologist, 81 n.

Milojčić, V., German prehistorian, 19 n.

Mining and quarrying, flint and stone, 80

Minns, E. H., British archaeologist, 117 n.

Mirrors, 117

Modes: metallurgy, 68; flint- and stone-working, 68–79

Molodova, Russia: paleolithic (mode 3) house site, 90, 91

Mongait, A. L., Russian archaeologist, 32 n.

Montespan, Grotte de, France, 139

Moon, observation of, 127, 128, 130, 131, 133

Moore, Henry, British sculptor, 123

Moral obligations, 143–145

Morgan, J. de, French archaeologist, 21

Morley, S. G.; Americanist, 129 n.

Morris, Desmond, British zoologist, 118–120

Mortillet, G. de: system for French prehistory, 26, 27; parochial nature of, 33

Mounds, burial, 137

Movius, Hallam, J., American prehistorian, 35 n., 65 n., 70 n., 73 n., 114 n.

Mugharet-es-skhul, Mt. Carmel, neanderthal burials, 114

Muller, Herbert, 47

Mulvaney, D. J., Australian prehistorian, 39 n., 69 n.

Mureybit, Syria, 93

Museums, 7, 9, 30, 31

Musical instruments, 118

Mycenae, Greece, 18

Myths: medium for enhancing group solidarity, 41 n.; reassurance of, 135, 138, 140 n.

Nationalism and archaeology: Europe, 6, 16; newly emergent states, 31. *See also* International effort

Natural order, 10, 11, 14

Natural selection: evolution of biological species, 13, 55; man profited by remaining biologically unspecialised, 56; operates on man through his cultural environment, notably through his economic system and technology, 61–63, 78, 89, 93, 95, 96, 101, 105; but also through noneconomic variables, 96; these include personal choice and deviance, 62, 98, 99, 111, 144; adaptive value of superior powers of objectification, 107; and of ecological discrimination, 126

Navigation, 43. *See also* Boats

Neanderthal man. *See Homo sapiens Neanderthalensis*

Nenquin, Jacques, Belgian prehistorian, 30 n.

Neolithic: definition, 15, 87; "revolution," 85–87

Index

Shaw, Thurston, British prehistorian, 78 n.

Shells, Spondylus, traffic, 139 n.

Sialk, Iran, French excavations, 22

Siberia, archaeological sites, 75, 76, 90 n.

Sipplingen, Germany, neolithic plant remains, 88

Society, human: tradition and historical awreness, 41; transmission of lore, 131; solidarity, 138; ceremonial centres, 143; obligations, 144, 145

Solecki, R., American prehistorian, 22, 94 n.

South Africa, 31, 65

Spain, 120, 122

Spears, paleolithic, wooden, 64–66, 84

Speech, articulate: social evolution, 62; outcome of capacity for objectification, 107, 108; for classifying environment, 108; context of appearance, 109; association with thought, 110; apes had no occasion to use it, 111; no valid osteological criteria, 112; lack of associated with restricted awareness of time, 125; characteristic of man, 143,145. *See also* Language.

Spencer, Baldwin, Australian ethnologist, 41 n.

Spengler, Oswald, 45, 46

Springs, veneration of, 139, 140

Stephens, John Lloyd, pioneer of Yucatan archaeology, 28

Stonehenge, England: described by Camden, 7; astronomical layout, 130–133

Stukeley, William, English antiquary, 13

Subsistence, 83–95. *See also* Agriculture; Farming; Hunting; Plant-gathering

Sudan Antiquities Service, 30

Sugihara, S., Japanese prehistorian, 75 n.

Sumerian civilization, 21, 22, 141, 142

Sun: lay-out of Maya monuments, 128–130; Stonehenge, 131–133; Teutonic mythology, 140 n.

Susa, Iran, French excavations, 21

Swadesh, M., American philologist, 113

Switzerland, 95 n., 139

Symbols: outcome of capacity for objectification, 107; role in defining groups and functions, 113; in art, 118–121, 140

Syria, 22, 93

Tanzania, prehistoric research, 31 n., 79, 84

Taylour, Lord William 18 n.

Technology: well represented in archaeology, 62; modes, 68–79; accompaniments of farming, 88, 89; progress, 97, 106. *See also* Flint and Stone; Metallurgy

Tehuacan, Mexico, evolution of domestic maize, 86 n., 92, 93

Tell Asmar, Iraq, American excavations, 22

Tell Halaf, Turkey, German excavations, 22

159

Index

Uruk, Iraq, German excavations, 141, 142
Ussher, Archbishop, 10–12, 14

Vallois, H. V., French paleontologist, 112 n.
Values, human: artificial, 49, 50; in economic life, 94, 97, 106; factor in behaviour, 144, 145
Ventris, Michael, British scholar, 18
Vernau, R., French prehistorian, 117 n.
Viaud, Gaston, French animal psychologist, 112, 124, 125
Vision, stereoscopic, 107

Wace, A. J. B., British archaeologist, 18, 140 n.
Walker, D. and Sieveking, Anne: early man in Malaya, 70 n.
Washburn, Sherwood L., American physical anthropologist: on feed-back between biological & socio-cultural behaviour, 57 n., 63
Watson, William, British sinologue, 24 n., 82 n.
Weapons, 57, 62, 64, 66, 84–86. *See also* spears
Weinberg, S. S., American archaeologist, 19 n.
Wendorf, Fred., American prehistorian, 36 n.
Wenner-Gren Foundation, New York, 35

Werner, A. G., German geologist, 11
Wheeler, R. E. M., British archaeologist, 78 n., 117 n.
Wik Monkan people, Cape York, Queensland, 108 n., 126
Willetts, William, British sinologue, 117 n.
Willey, Gordon R., Americanist, 79 n., 141 n.
Winther, J., Danish prehistorian, 140 n.
Woolley, Leonard, British archaeologist, 137
World prehistory, 5, 15, 26–28, 34–38
World view of human history, 1–52 *passim*, especially 34–38, 47–51
Wormington, Marie, American prehistorian, 38 n.
Worship, 135, 140
Writing: storage of information, 62; diversity, 100; cultural feedback, 110; inscriptions, 130. *See also* Literacy; Scripts

Yale University, 36 n.
Young, J. Z., British biologist, 110 n.

Zamiatnin, S. N., Russian prehistorian, 89 n.
Zeist, W. van, Dutch botanist, 93 n.

161